⚭ *The* ⚭

LEADERSHIP
GENIUS OF
*J*ESUS

Ancient
Wisdom
for
Modern
Business

WILLIAM BEAUSAY II

THOMAS NELSON PUBLISHERS
Nashville

Published in Nashville, Tennessee, by Thomas Nelson, Inc.

Library of Congress Cataloging-in-Publication Data
Beausay, William, 1957–
    The leadership genius of Jesus / William Beausay II.
        p.   cm.
    ISBN 0-7852-7165-1 (hc)
    1. Christian leadership. 2. Jesus Christ—Leadership.
I. Title.
BV652.1.B377 1998
262'.1—dc21   97–38372
                                                          CIP

Printed in the United States of America.
1 2 3 4 5 6 BVG 02 01 00 99 98

Contents

Thanks

This book would not be in your hands without the efforts of many great friends. First, thanks to my publisher, Victor Oliver. Everyone should be fortunate enough to spend ten minutes with this man. It would forever alter their perception of excellence in action. Thank you, Vic, for your leadership and direction in this project. Thanks as well to the indispensable and charming Rose Marie Sroufe; Brian Hampton, managing editor of Oliver-Nelson and wordsmith without peer; and the entire supporting cast at Thomas Nelson Publishers.

Special thanks as well to my agent, Sara Fortenberry, my brother and friend, Mike Beausay, Bill Bullard, John Ulmer, Jack Helmer, Gary Brown, Steve Milanowski, and my mom and dad for your friendship, support, insight, and many, many laughs!

To my kids, Jake, Jessie, and Zac: You guys are my passion, and I love you all. Be leaders wherever you go, but above all be like Jesus.

Finally, to Kathi, my fearless leader and best friend, thank you. I love you.

For information on Bill Beausay's
- speaking availability
- training workshops
- print, audio, video, and software products,
  call him at
  > (419) 893-1983

or write him at
  > P.O. Box 4444
  > Maumee, OH 43537

or E-mail him at
  > bbeausay@aol.com

The Power of One

One is a powerful number.

Nobody who has seen it will forget a short clip from the movie *City Slickers*. Curly, the creaky, rawhide-tough cowboy trail boss, is sharing the secret of life with his urban protégé, played by comedian Billy Crystal. After challenging his young client to name the key to life, Curly holds up one finger and stares into Crystal's eyes.

After a long pause, he squints and croaks simply, "One thing."

Leadership always boils down to *singularity:* one person doing one thing. Few things in life excite me more than seeing what one person fully committed to one thing can accomplish. Whether it's great people leading great nations, managers leading teams, teachers leading students, or parents leading homes, remarkable things begin to happen when one person focuses his effort.

Jesus' style was the epitome of one. Once some Pharisees were hotly contesting his claims to godliness, his wanton disregard for keeping the Sabbath, and his insinuations that they were blind. They made the mistake of questioning him on this.

Can you boil your mission down to one thing?

Jesus' reply to them was sharp—a perfect illustration of his one thing: "The thief does not come except to steal, and to kill, and to destroy. I have come that they may have life, and that they may have it more abundantly" (John 10:10 NKJV).

Jesus' one thing served him well. His tart comment based on a simple motive pierced to the heart of the Pharisees' prejudices and misconceptions. Such a simple, beguiling style—focusing on one thing.

What's your one thing? Do you need to spend some time finding it?

Five Leadership Myths

I once knew a man with tremendous leadership potential. He was a salesman for a chemical company, and I needed his help leading a project I was managing. He was perfect: self-motivated, able to focus on tasks, effective with people, a quick problem solver, and a motivator.

There was only one glaring problem: He didn't believe in himself. The word *leadership* terrorized him. To him, *leadership* had transcendent magic to which only a select few people held the elixir. Unfortunately, he believed a suicidal mixture of leadership mythology.

In their wonderful book *Leaders*, Warren Bennis and Burt Nanus take aim at five key myths many of us have come to believe.

1. Leadership is a rare skill. Nothing could be farther from reality. Literally, wherever two or more are gathered, a leader will emerge. Leadership is always up for grabs, and it's a common human trait to assume it.

2. Leaders are born, not made. Few real leaders are pedigreed. What generates leadership is a complex human process full of trial and error, victories and defeats, insights, intuitions, and always a dynamic confluence of events. Rarely is it from natural endowment.

Effective leadership is not what you think.

3. Leaders are charismatic. Though charismatic people may be thrust into leadership roles, most of the greatest leaders in history have been quiet, even shy individuals. So are many of the effective everyday leaders in our lives.

4. Leadership exists only at the top of an organization. Given the nature of human beings, this statement cannot be true. Everyone needs leadership delivered in an up close and personal manner.

5. Leaders control, direct, prod, and manipulate. Leaders transform people and events. They make things happen by engaging people and drawing them into a specific enterprise. Almost all effective leaders use means other than brute force or threat. They almost always lead by relying on encouragement, counsel, wisdom, and personal challenge.

Jesus was one of the greatest leaders of all time. He shattered all these myths. For example, he downplayed his leadership, and he told his disciples they would do even greater things than he. He was born into the home of a humble craftsman, hardly Ivy League material. Though he had charisma, he simply encouraged others to do as they saw him doing. Jesus didn't rule from atop a mighty fortress of lower-level employees, and never was he a pushy whip-cracker.

Had you asked him the key to success, I doubt he would have said "time management" or "dressing for success." He didn't have a daily planner, and if he created a strategic plan, nobody ever saw it. In short, his leadership style broke all the molds and altered the course of the world in the process. Beware of the myths of leadership that may shackle you.

Filaments

Mark Twain, in explaining his exuberance and wit to a reporter, declared, "I was born excited." Unfortunately, we're not all born excited. Come to think of it, many of us are pretty dull. I know one super-dull fellow. Bring up sports, and his eyes glaze over. Talk about making money, and his body goes limp. Talk philosophy, and he stares blankly. Tell a joke, and he grins weakly. The guy is a certified dud.

Until you talk astronomy.

Mention quasars, and he lights up like one. Talk about life on Mars, and suddenly, there is life in him! Mention gamma ray bursts from distant black holes, and the black holes in his face flicker to life.

We all have filaments that glow under different conditions. When our filaments burn brightly, life is exciting, edgy, fun, hopeful, and satisfying.

Leaders have high-intensity filaments, and they know what makes them glow. They also know how to ignite themselves, and they are comfortable bathing others with their unique brilliance.

Jesus used the metaphor of luminance to describe many things. He understood that certain people have a

What makes you glow inside?

brightly burning filament within them, and they owe it to themselves to let it shine.

Once, among a group of religious teachers, Jesus remarked, "I am the light of the world. He who follows Me shall not walk in darkness, but have the light of life" (John 8:12 NKJV).

His brashness incensed the Pharisees. "You can't brag about yourself and expect us to believe it just because you say it!" they scolded.

"I know where I came from and where I am going," he replied. "You *do not know* where I come from and *where I am going*" (John 8:14 NKJV, emphasis added).

It has been said that there is more variation among leaders than themes, but of this element I'm certain: *Leaders know where they're going*. They know what makes them excited, and they are bold in sharing it.

What excites you? What makes you incandescent on the inside? Don't let anyone, not even learned and influential people, snuff it out.

Blind Groping

When I speak to large groups at night, I occasionally do a mixer that everyone finds entertaining. I randomly divide people into one of four groups: horses, cows, chickens, and pigs. They're given these instructions: When the lights go off and it's pitch-black, start making the noise that your animal makes as loudly as you can. When you find someone else making the same noise, link arms with the person, and search for other roving clusters.

When the lights are doused, the fun begins. You can imagine the whinnies and wails of Clydesdales, bovines, poultry, and pork. Most people just wander around yelling. It's funny! When the lights are turned back on, we do a quick show of hands to discover which group of animals was most successful in making connections.

Life can be like this audio barnyard. We're all groping around blindly in the darkness of life trying to find what works for us. We're looking for people, careers, hobbies, lifestyles, habits, and so forth like a person blindly groping in a room full of options. We can't see what's available, yet we're choosing the best we can. Every once in a while the lights flicker a bit, and we're able to see, for better or worse, the matchups we've chosen.

Uncommon leaders reorient the disoriented.

Some of us don't like what we've picked. For example, we're disillusioned with the people we've picked for mates or friends, our careers are disappointing, our hobbies seem empty, our lifestyles suddenly show themselves to be the sources of trouble rather than satisfaction, and some of our habits become self-defeating. Some of us conclude that all this choosing in the dark is futile, and we lose hope, spending our time mooing and oinking our way around in ignorance. And nobody reaches out to lend us a hand.

Jesus did an interesting thing when he noticed that people were disoriented or frightened or had given up on themselves: He made valiant efforts to grab them. He never allowed the darkness or apparent confusion of the moment to stifle his search for good people lost in a disoriented life.

One time Jesus was eating with a group of prostitutes, alcoholics, and corrupt politicians. Gropers. He told them three stories about lost things: a sheep, some silver coins, and a runaway heir to a fortune. In all cases Jesus made it clear that finding what was lost was cause for celebration!

Jesus didn't just talk about this; he did it. Rather than harshly ignore or scold seekers, he beckoned them and gave them a firm mooring. He incited faith, not fear or humiliation, in the gropers.

People around you are groping for leadership, direction, wisdom, help, and friendship. Learn to recognize the bleat of a lost sheep or the cry of a desperate runaway. Boldly give them whatever wisdom and direction you have. That's what good leaders do.

Danger Zones

Leadership rarely arises without the recognition of some danger or impending trouble. Leadership seems to ignite itself under these conditions. It's amazing to me how certain people, often the ones you'd least expect, step forward to lead in dire emergencies. Threatening circumstances reveal the true leaders.

The problem is that most threats in our lives are not obvious. For example, the threat of marital dissolution is ever present, and in some cases is tacitly sanctioned by society. Financial ruin lurks behind every new credit card we receive. Our ability to think independently and creatively slips quietly past with each hour of television we watch. We often teeter on the edge of disaster and don't even know it.

As radical as it sounds, clearly observed dangers help people find lives worth *leading*. Illustrations are everywhere. Take these examples that I drew out of my local newspaper today:

• Families are falling apart at record rates. For years, we naively assumed that our family relationships were a certainty, a given. Once a society loses a sense of threat in regard to the home, its members become complacent, and household leaders stop leading. That's exactly what's

---

Threatening circumstances reveal leaders.

occurred. Divorce and family splintering shouldn't be surprising.

• Studies show that fewer than 25 percent of workers feel they're working at their full potential, 50 percent don't put forth any more effort than is required to hold on to a job, and 75 percent say they could be more effective than they are. All human organizations suffer with unmotivated people. I suspect the adage is true that "companies pay employees just enough so they won't quit, and the employees work just hard enough so they won't get fired."

Workers like these don't see any threat. They don't sense that their jobs are exposed and threatened daily. They don't see how perilously close their corporations and businesses are to failure unless they give 100 percent effort. They fail to perceive that without their vigilant effort, the whole structure collapses. Ergo, nobody steps forward to lead them to higher plateaus of effort.

• A local high school is being overrun by violence. Nobody does much beyond having token counseling sessions with "troubled" youths and hoisting STOP VIOLENCE banners here and there. "Kids will be kids," claim hapless parents unencumbered with imagination or fresh ideas.

Then a Hispanic boy gets knifed in broad daylight between classes. Suddenly, the always present threat shows up in the form of a bleeding, slumped body. The danger is recognized, leaders arise, and major change gets under way.

Will the change continue in this school? It depends on how visible the threat remains. Threatened people stay on their toes.

Jesus led people within a deeply dangerous situation. Threats of death, stoning, public rebuke, military reprisal, and starvation were daily concerns. Such threats didn't cause his team to shudder; rather, they struck harder, often at the focal point of the threats: temple officials and the political establishment. Jesus didn't allow the danger zones of his day to alter his plans. He came because of the danger zones.

There are threats to your life today. Be aware of their presence, though in most cases they'll be hard to see. Once you find them, strike hard and fast with courageous vision, brave words, and tough action. You must do this immediately.

My Leader Board

When I first began this book, I made a list of the leaders in my life. I entitled the list "My Leader Board," and on it I wrote the names of pivotal people in my life, the real difference makers. I tried not to define *leader* any closer than that, preferring to make a general list from which I could compare and contrast.

Several things struck me. First, most of the people on my list were never official leaders. By that, I mean that most of them never had authority over me (like a teacher, coach, boss, or manager). They were people I chose to follow and respect.

Second, I actively compared myself to them. My leaders were not individuals who dealt orders but ones who had qualities I wanted for myself. By their actions and lifestyles, they proved that a higher level of life was possible for me and, with some work, within my grasp.

Third, I knew I was important to these people. They felt I had value, and they freely gave me input and advice.

I suggest that you create a list for yourself. Select five to ten of your life leaders, and write their names here. See if the qualities of the people on your list are similar to the qualities of the people on my list.

What kind of people do you follow?

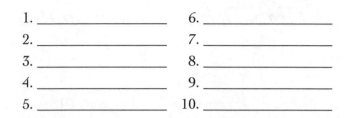

1. _____   6. _____
2. _____   7. _____
3. _____   8. _____
4. _____   9. _____
5. _____   10. _____

Had we been able to ask the followers of Jesus to make a leader board at the ends of their lives, there is little doubt who would be in first position. Jesus' words had profound impact; his stories, riveting life; his presence, an unforgettable, life-changing aura.

I've always found it interesting how relaxed those considered "sinners" were in Jesus' presence and conversely how uncomfortable those considered "religious" were. The difference was due in part to the fact that he never forced himself on people or grandstanded for effect. His leadership secret was the depth of his caring for every individual with whom he spent time.

Remember the specific qualities you've admired and benefited from in the past. Then pass them on. In Jesus' words, "If you've done them to the least of these, you've done them to me."

A High-Definition Personality

I once interviewed a former CIA "spook." He was a Vietnam vet who became a spy in the aftermath of a distinguished military career that included a harrowing POW experience.

As you can imagine, this conversation was fascinating, but one element stood out: *If you were to place this man in a roomful of people, he is the last guy you'd ever expect to be a spy*. I had a wild notion that I'd be interviewing a Steven Seagal knockoff, complete with trench coat, sunglasses, and an Uzi strapped to his leg. I expected him to come down out of the heating ducts dangling on wires, with James Bond music playing in the background.

Was I ever wrong. My guy was smallish and balding with thick glasses and a serious demeanor.

My silly disappointment evaporated almost immediately. The gentleman had what I call a high-definition personality. Under his plain persona was a distinct man, clear and lucid. He spoke with alacrity and depth, and something about his commanding gaze made it hard for me to look away. He had clear thoughts, unusual opinions, and clever arguments. He filled the space between us with life—the

---

Seek to be a high-resolution individual.

kind of energy flowing from a person who knows exactly who he is and where he is going.

Jesus was like that. Throughout his career, he was able on many occasions to slip around unnoticed. But when he spoke, people stopped and listened. His personality was highly defined and compelling, indelible in a way many listeners had never experienced.

In your efforts to become a better leader, focus your effort on the qualities that make you clear and highly defined in other people's eyes: solid eye contact, a command of the language, sound logic, firm opinions, openness, articulate expression of the things you believe, and knowledge of where you're going and why others should follow you.

Rather than smooth yourself out, define yourself.

No Paths

We're all familiar with adages and admonitions about following the least traveled path. This is good advice. However, on occasion there is no path at all.

There's a story of a World War II field commander who was leading a group of American soldiers in hot pursuit of a renegade German platoon. The German soldiers were retreating rapidly through a mountain pass and needed to be engaged and eliminated as quickly as possible. As the small American detachment ascended the mountain pass, the trail suddenly opened onto an open field booby-trapped with mines. Night was falling, so the commander ordered his men to make camp in the shallow woods at the edge of the field.

The next morning they arose to discover that a beautiful blanket of snow had fallen during the night. The impact of the weather immediately struck them as they contemplated the danger of trying to negotiate a snow-covered minefield.

The commander walked to the edge of the field and assessed the situation. Turning to his men, he said, "We have no choice but to send one man out across the field. Should he be so unfortunate as to lose his life on a mine,

---

Make a way.

the next man will follow his steps as far as he can, then change course and strike out on his own. We'll keep this up until we have safe footprints across the field."

Then the commander turned and started walking across the field. Shocked, one of his junior officers grabbed him by the shoulder, saying, "Sir, you can't go first! Who will lead us if you die?"

The commander turned to him and said with a smile, "Why, you will, of course." Then he began his walk across the minefield.

Forty-five minutes later, the commander arrived safely on the opposite side of the field. Turning again to his men, he yelled, "Just follow my footsteps and you will be completely safe."

Where Jesus was leading his people there were no paths. But that was no reason to retreat. Jesus' leadership was based on the premise that if there is no trail, make one. And just to keep it interesting, make the hard one yourself.

You needn't be a wild-eyed rogue to be a fearless leader. Simply find a difficult problem, and lead through it. You can easily find one today. Many people are waiting for a hero like you to emerge. Chances are good that you won't be blown to smithereens, so go on.

What Grips You?

Not long ago I heard Michael Jordan interviewed on *Oprah*. She asked him point-blank, "What's it like, Michael, to be living your dreams and doing all that you've ever wanted?"

Michael Jordan, reflecting on his childhood passion, replied, "This isn't my dream, Oprah. My dream was to play pro baseball. It wasn't until I gave up that dream and did what I was made to do that all this happened."

Now learn this truth: Some people have ambitions, and others have destiny. A few have both in unity. What distinguishes people unified with themselves is not the grandiosity of their visions, *but what grips them as a result of seeing something with pristine clarity.* The real leaders are not people with grand plans, but people with a vision so clear that it can't be ignored.

What visions gripped Jesus? What moved him? What made him get out of bed in the morning? What kept him up late at night?

He offered several glimpses to his disciples. He revealed one of the brightest shortly before his arrest. Jesus said, "These things I have spoken to you, that My joy may

---

Do you have any visions so clear that you can't possibly ignore them?

remain in you, and that your joy may be full. . . . No longer do I call you servants, for a servant does not know what his master is doing; but I have called you friends, for all things that I heard from My Father I have made known to you" (John 15:11, 15 NKJV). Jesus' ambition and destiny were about revealing the true source of joy.

For three dazzling years, Jesus was gripped by the combination of ambition and destiny. What grips you so tightly that it will still be effervescent and vibrant in three years? Today, begin the search for what electrifies you. Enjoy the sense of courage and confidence it provides. Then with a vision so clear that you can touch it, share it with your friends.

Titles and Deeds

Let me tell you about the worst boss I ever saw. He was given authority prematurely, and he abused it wildly. He harshly ordered people when he should have gently directed. He bullied people when he should have asked nicely. He whispered when he should have screamed. He delegated poorly, and then he naively chose people who were as inept as he was. He had the title of leader, but he had no idea about how to lead, much less a deed that proved his leadership abilities.

I can speak harshly about this guy with some authority: *He was me!* I thought I was leading, but in reality nobody was following. I was the proverbial boy leading the parade; I had the title and position but no ability. As I marched through town, the parade turned down a side street, and oblivious to everything, I marched happily on.

Some of us labor under leaders with bequeathed authority, none of it earned. Others of us have had the unique opportunity to serve under leaders who have earned their rank. When those people speak, you listen. Their honesty, opinions, and directions have clout and power. Their presence creates a forceful inertia rather than stubborn resistance.

Lead by your actions.

Leaders who have won the position by their deeds are easy to follow. Titular leaders, on the other hand, are very easy to second-guess and defy.

Jesus led by his deeds. He had no legal mandate, no political cronies, no rich uncles, and no connections outside the local lumberyard. All he had was the authority granted to him by God.

The people he led were an interesting crowd. They weren't a bunch of bored guys in letter jackets hanging around waiting for some action. They all had jobs, responsibilities, and obligations. They had strong ties to their own towns, and some had wives and families. Yet by his deeds, Jesus persuaded them to leave homes and careers and follow him.

Ask yourself this question: What kind of person would cause me to leave home today? Not a leader by title, I guarantee, but a leader so compelling, you couldn't justify staying home.

Good leadership cannot be purchased, bequeathed, or willed. Followers won't follow that. Effective leaders have earned the position by performance. Today, be a leader by your deeds: honest and credible by example, strong and sound in your opinions, temperate and wise in your judgment. Earn by your action something nobody can take from you: the deed of leadership.

Servant Leadership

Servant leadership is a leadership style that has gained tremendous popularity. What's so odd about servant leadership is that it seems like an oxymoron. Aren't servants and leaders polar opposites? I'm certain you've seen examples of servant leadership but may not have known what you were seeing.

I spoke with a true servant leader when I was consulting for a major petroleum refiner. Two men approached me—a high-level manager and a line worker at the refinery. Though the manager wouldn't consider himself a leader, what he did certifies his position.

The refinery worker said, "Several years ago, management asked for ideas to make this place more efficient. I had an idea, but I also had a problem. A small secret. I'd worked here since I dropped out of school, and I couldn't read or write. Even though I had a great idea, I couldn't write it down. So I stayed quiet."

The story was getting interesting, so I urged him on.

"Well, this man [pointing to the manager] made the difference. He was the person who asked for new ideas. I trusted him. I also trusted that he wouldn't laugh at me

Servanthood: leadership in elemental form.

when I presented my idea written by my ten-year-old granddaughter.

"Not only didn't he laugh, but he said, 'How can I help you?'"

The rest is history. The manager encouraged the line worker by asking him the question common to servant leaders: "How can I help?" He also went the extra mile to encourage the man to finish his GED and even take college-level courses at a nearby community college.

Servant leadership was the core of Jesus' style. We see it reflected in the actions of his followers. His disciples were not docile little robots. They were human beings with problems and cares and worries. They often asked him for help. They needed guidance and clearly felt comfortable approaching him for personal support.

Jesus knew his servant leadership was different. To illustrate that, he compared his example to more traditional leadership: "You know that in this world kings are tyrants, and officials lord it over the people beneath them. But among you it should be quite different. Whoever wants to be a leader among you must be your servant" (Matt. 20:25–26 NLT).

Are your subordinates at ease with you? Don't "lord" yourself over them. Furthermore, drop the "what's in it for me?" agenda. Take the radical, maybe even unprecedented step of serving others in ways you think they'll appreciate. They'll follow you for it.

SWOTs

One trait shared by all leaders is the ability to make shrewd observations. Savvy leaders use their vision to pierce the fog of the future. An effective tool for reducing the fog and developing crow's nest vision is analyzing SWOTs.

SWOT is a business school acronym for strengths, weaknesses, opportunities, and threats. Whereas managers can survive without understanding these four concerns, they are indispensable information to successful leaders.

Strengths. Leaders must have an ongoing awareness of which followers have specific strengths or which products or service lines are particularly strong. It also helps if leaders sense how the strengths unite or dilute one another.

Weaknesses. In the same way leaders must understand strengths, they must know as precisely as possible where weaknesses lie. It's practically impossible to lead successfully without candidly and swiftly admitting the points of greatest weakness in people, products, services, and themselves as leaders.

Know what you're looking ahead for.

Opportunities. Certain people present opportunities that others do not. This is true within families, businesses, church groups, and communities. Good leaders sense opportunities that exist within each unique individual in their sphere and the potential matchups of people that can create strength and stability.

Threats. Leaders must have a sense of threats. They must know their people and the specific threats that could derail or discourage the ranks. They must also be able to successfully communicate the nature of the threats to followers.

Jesus was a SWOT guy. He knew who his strong people were, and he spent time building, teaching, and encouraging them. Jesus knew the weaknesses in several of his disciples. He predicted that some followers would find his teaching too hard and walk away. They did.

Opportunities? Jesus was active in seizing ongoing events and watching carefully how pieces of his life puzzle united. He appeared to never tire of watching for hot spots. Threats? Jesus was immersed in a swirling stew of rules, traditions, political pressure, legal constraints, and popularity. Though his focus was on larger matters, he was careful to know and plan for the threats that continually shadowed him and his disciples.

Use this SWOT template to think and look forward. These four divisions of assessment allow you to sharply define where you must place your effort in proactively leading your life and the lives of others.

☞ 13 ☜

Critics

I've found it to be true that any radical new idea passes through three phases: (1) the *opposition phase*, in which the new idea is laughed off and swiftly dismissed as ludicrous; (2) the *ridicule phase*, in which the new idea and its supporters are hotly criticized and mocked despite growing popularity; and (3) the *self-evident phase* when the idea is finally considered so brilliant that any moron could immediately recognize its value.

Some critics will decry and dismiss every suggestion a leader or innovator makes. These critics often have logic, precedence, and certified proof that your plans are wacky. Just for fun, let's allow some critics to explain in their own words some of the things *they knew to be true:*

Airplanes are interesting toys but of no military value. (Maréchal Ferdinand Foch, professor of strategy, École Supérieure de Guerre)

Louis Pasteur's theory of germs is ridiculous fiction. (Pierre Pachet, professor of physiology at Toulouse, 1872)

The abdomen, the chest, and the brain will forever be shut from the intrusion of the wise and humane surgeon.

Few things are as certain as criticism.

(Sir John Eric Erichsen, British surgeon, appointed Surgeon Extraordinary to Queen Victoria, 1873)

Computers in the future may weigh no more than 1.5 tons. (*Popular Mechanics*, 1949)

I have traveled the length and breadth of this country and talked with the best people, and I can assure you that data processing is a fad that won't last out the year. (The editor in charge of business books for Prentice Hall, 1957)

I'm just glad it'll be Clark Gable who's falling on his face and not Gary Cooper. (Gary Cooper on his decision not to take the leading role in *Gone with the Wind*)

We don't like their sound, and guitar music is on the way out. (Decca Recording Co. rejecting the Beatles, 1962)

Stocks have reached what looks like a permanently high plateau. (Irving Fisher, professor of economics, Yale University, 1929)

Drill for oil? You mean drill into the ground to try and find oil? You're crazy. (Drillers whom Edwin L. Drake tried to enlist to his project to drill for oil in 1859)

The concept is interesting and well-formed, but in order to earn better than a "C," the idea must be feasible. (A Yale University management professor in response to Fred Smith's paper proposing reliable overnight delivery service; Smith went on to found Federal Express Corp.)

Had Jesus submitted his plan in writing to the teachers and authorities of the day, he'd have been fortunate not to have been immediately flunked or flogged. His entire endeavor was fraught with opposition and ridicule from the first day to the last. The self-evident phase didn't even appear until after he was crucified! Yet in following his own certainty, he launched a movement that has grown steadily to this day.

It was Jesus' style to proceed relentlessly past the critics and onward toward his nonperishable vision. You can too.

Dangerous People

All men dream, but not equally. Those who dream by night in the dusty recesses of their minds awake to find it was vanity. But the dreamers of the day are dangerous men, that they may act their dreams with open eyes to make it possible." I love this quote by T. E. Lawrence. I meet a lot of successful people. I look for them. I've noticed two levels. People at the first level are casually successful; they have worked hard, and they enjoy the fruits of their efforts. Then there's the second tier of truly unusual winners: They're on fire for something. Their mission is intense and personal.

The steely eyed dreamers whose eyes don't shift and whose will won't quiver are "dangerous." Jesus tried to recruit people like that. He knew the visions he had predicted were daring. His followers would need to be "dangerous" to meet the challenges.

Jesus tried to develop that dangerous streak in his followers. The way in which he did so was a clinic in leadership development.

One of the intriguing elements of Jesus' leadership style was that he dealt with people where they were. It's

---

Be dangerous.

rare to find a situation where he didn't (1) start conversations with people about something happening at that time and (2) urge them to push an element of themselves farther.

Let's look at his first contact with several people. How about the Samaritan woman at the well? He asked her for a drink. His first followers? He asked them why they were following him. The widow whose only son died in the village of Nain? He comforted her.

His first contact was always followed by an appeal to stretch to a higher level of faith. To the woman at the well came the suggestion to seek "living water." To his first disciples came the suggestion to, by faith, join in the adventure of a lifetime. To the widow at Nain came the challenge of faith and then the restored life of her dead boy.

Dangerous leaders make bold suggestions for the lives of others. They do so by easy, natural first contact followed by a riveting, encouraging call to stretch. You can use these two dangerous steps today. Join with the people following you, then nudge them onward.

Accountability

Keeping leaders accountable is always tricky business. On the one hand, leaders are implicitly trusted to protect the common good and make sound decisions driven by a leaderly perspective. We voluntarily submit ourselves to their better judgment and follow them in faith. Yet on the other hand, leaders must answer to someone should their decisions harm the welfare of others.

Jesus' all-volunteer disciple army was not always happy with what he was doing. Jesus uniquely handled the breach of understanding by *practicing mutual accountability to a higher purpose*. Jesus loved being obedient to God in heaven. Therefore, he spent enormous amounts of time grooming a similar love of obedience in his followers. Keeping all of them, himself included, aimed at that larger purpose created mutual accountability.

A good example of this unique dynamic happened when he returned from a trip to the mountains with Peter, James, and John. The other disciples had failed in healing a boy while Jesus was gone, and they were desperate to discover why. Jesus replied in a way that reoriented them

> *Be collectively accountable to a higher standard.*

toward the thing to which they were mutually accountable. "You didn't have enough faith," he said plainly. "If you have the faith of a mustard seed, you can move mountains. Nothing would be impossible for you." This was the standard that everyone on the team needed to reach.

Most of us are enmeshed in some form of top-down accountability. Either we're in the top spot, or we answer directly to someone who is. Have you taken the time to know what your higher goal is as a group of people? Have you clarified where you are leading your team or asked your superior about where you're all going? This exercise puts the genius of Jesus to work for you today.

"Make Me Feel Special"

One of the most remarkable leaders of our day is businesswoman Mary Kay Ash, founder of Mary Kay Cosmetics. Her story is an inspiration, her life worth examining. She has said her key to working with people is imagining they're wearing a placard that says, "Make me feel special." She proceeds to make them feel special in any way she can, and her success certifies her leadership advice.

I want you to imagine walking into your job today dedicated to the belief that *you accomplish being the best you can be by helping others be their best*. I know, it sounds unnatural and just about the last thing you'd ever decide to do. It feels more normal to look out for yourself and phooey on everyone else. Many of us are selfish this way.

The practice of giving to others what they need to succeed is *pure Jesus*. He constantly reminded his followers to give themselves to one another without hesitation or guile. The difficulty of the lesson was magnified by the fact that it ran against their competitive nature (as it does today). Thus, Jesus had to deal with disciples whose only goal seemed to be winning his favor rather than serving one another.

Help others be their personal best.

Jesus handled the situation in unique form. Not only did he tell them to submit themselves to one another, but he demonstrated the concept repeatedly (much to the utter amazement of his followers). Jesus washed his disciples' feet, made them meals, invited them to come to dinner parties, personally provided food, and performed many other services. He made them feel pretty special.

Are you really interested in people? Modeling Jesus' leadership style means generously giving yourself to those below you on the influence ladder. Most people aren't treated nicely by superiors, so they will notice any effort you make in that direction. Sometimes the most powerful strokes of leadership are the ones that speak for themselves.

Preparation

I like Abraham Lincoln's wise perspective on preparation. He said, "If I had ten hours to cut down a tree, I'd spend the first eight sharpening my ax."

A very wealthy man I know was asked by a group of students how he amassed his fortune. His reply was simple: "I plan half the day, and I work the other half."

A buzz raced through the small group as they dreamed of how they would apply the easy plan. "Imagine, four glorious hours of planning, then a mere four hours of labor!"

The rich man abruptly nipped their dreams. "I didn't mean I plan four hours and work four hours a day," he declared. *"I plan twelve hours, then work twelve hours!"*

Few things are as sacred to modern leaders as adequate preparation. What do they prepare for? Usually, it boils down to managing time, optimizing their attitude, and developing on-task focus. All great leaders seem to have found a system to initiate and monitor these elements.

Ask ten leaders about their system and you'll get ten different replies. Technology in the form of calendars, flowcharts, and strategic plans aids the cause, but the bottom line of preparation is always a thread called

---

The future is coming; are you ready?

self-discipline: one solitary person making himself or herself review and plan what's going to happen next.

Jesus' method of preparing was uniquely his own. As in most other arenas of leadership, he had his own style. We see reference after reference in the Bible about Jesus departing from the crowd to be alone. His disciples said he prayed and meditated. By his own admission he observed what God was doing, and he fasted. For the most part nobody really knows what else he did, but this much is certain: When he returned, he was a dynamo.

Emulating his style requires several key steps. Depart from the crowds daily. Think, meditate, and pray if you like. See clearly where you're going today. Set aside a disciplined time of diligent thinking and planning. Learn to let the moments of solitude focus you and energize you. Then attack your day prepared, and in the style of Jesus, make others the beneficiaries of your preparation.

Coolness and Conspicuous Courage

 We value coolness and courage for two reasons. First, they're practical for navigating the often frightening oceans of life. Second, they're rare. You can probably count on one hand people who possess them.

Most people who are unusually cool under pressure have no idea how they do it. Through experience, they've learned that coolness under pressure is a function not of thinking, but of acting.

Gen. Douglas MacArthur was a case in point. He was a leadership icon, a military hero without peer. A more highly decorated wartime commander this country has never produced. Though he distinguished himself repeatedly throughout his life, MacArthur was at his zenith when he was a young colonel in France during World War I. *He won nine Silver Stars for bravery under fire.* He eventually added the Distinguished Service Cross for his "coolness and conspicuous courage."

To MacArthur, coolness and courage were not attributes to be discussed. As most great leaders would agree, those qualities were automatic by-products of

Relax and remember who marches with you.

action-oriented leadership. No fancy phrases or concepts were useful in doing the hard work of leadership. This simplicity fueled MacArthur's trademark coolness and courage.

Jesus was cucumber cool. He had the allure and ease of a man who knew exactly where he was going. Like other great leaders, he never mentioned self-confidence. *Unlike other great leaders,* he directed listeners to the focus of his strength.

What was that direction? Early in his ministry, Jesus gave a long talk in which he laid out many of the basics of his mission. He encouraged listeners not to worry too much about their lives. God, he assured them, valued each of them so much that if they would seek him first, he would give them everything. Everything.

Do you maintain self-control in testing circumstances? It's difficult to get rattled if you dedicate yourself to seeking God first. Jesus' motivation was not a craving for valor or accolades. His point was to pursue a campaign of action with the full confidence that God marched at his side, come what may. Remarkable calm accrues to leaders engulfed and energized by the right accompaniment. Know who marches at your flank.

❧ 19 ❧

Deploy Yourself

I did some consulting with a successful company known for its ability to wisely delegate management responsibility. Naturally, I wondered how such a reputation was earned, so I asked. The CEO, an affable and visionary woman, was delighted to tell me but warned it was way too simple to be of any value in a book.

I laughed at the thought. I've come to appreciate that many great insights first appear as humble understatements.

She told me that she tried many ways to delegate tasks but completely failed. She decided to try something new. She began with the recognition that nobody understands the world exactly as you see it. Therefore, others don't understand or value directions and matters delegated to them the same way you do. To be successful in deploying your limited resources as a leader, you need to make sure that followers see what you see as you see it.

Her technique for showing others her perspective was as graceful as that of a bulldozer: Every time you must delegate something, she said, *ask four times for it to be done.*

That was it! In her estimation, leaders were responsible for what their followers saw. Her method of choice to make that happen was to ask for what she wanted four

---

Delegate wisely.

different times and in four different ways. Based on that, she reckoned, her staff would be alerted to her seriousness, focused on her mission, and poised to think for themselves.

Oh, yes. She was meticulous about follow-through, and her people understood exactly what she wanted.

I think Jesus knew he would never be able to create carbon copies of himself. He knew that to drill his people on special words and phrases would make them nothing more than empty-headed parrots. The world didn't need people like that.

Since delegation was part of his mission, he decided to do something new. He devoted himself to building pass-along value in his disciples. Jesus demonstrated to his disciples how to pass on the good things they received. Passing along goodness proved to be a potent means of deploying himself.

His parable of the talents summarized his pass-it-on philosophy. Three men were given talents (money) to manage for a rich man. One man invested his talents and made a fortune. The second man invested his and made a smaller wad. But the third man buried his talents in a hole. When the rich man returned, he heaped praise on the first two, but had only scorn for the third. Within the story we see that the whole ministry of Jesus was oriented toward passing along, deploying if you will, the rich gift of God's love.

Make an investment in people today. Whatever you are most gifted in, give it away to others. Then encourage them to pass it along to someone else. It's not only a great way to deploy yourself, but also a great way to see your leadership efforts multiply exponentially.

Decision Making

Every moment of life offers options. We're all constantly making decisions that affect ourselves and others. I think we'd all agree that some of our decisions are more important than others. For instance, you can decide to work less today, shave your head and get a tattoo, or become a vegetarian. On the other hand, your board of directors can decide to replace you, your boss can decide to promote you, or your spouse can decide to leave you.

Decisions fuel the drama of life.

A key attribute of effective leaders is their awareness of the gravity of their choices. Never has there been a great leader who was not conscious of the decisions going on around him or her all the time. Even the most vile demagogue sees the impact of decisions. All great leaders sculpt the future using decision making as a chisel.

Jesus had unusual rules for making his decisions. Rather than make choices based on comfort and gain (as most of us do), Jesus made decisions based upon whether or not the outcome would serve God, serve people, or fulfill a prophecy. He was a reckless servant–decision maker.

If this rule system doesn't appear to have any real value to modern leaders, think again. We do most of our

---

Decisions fuel the drama of life.

daily decision making casually. We hardly give most decisions a second thought. *Emulating Jesus' style is no more difficult than upgrading each decision by thinking of the person(s) it will best serve.* If that happens to be you and your one-sided wants, get comfortable being unlike Jesus. However, if you can honestly say that your choices serve others and the long-term legacy you've mapped for yourself, proceed with total abandon. Keep making decisions with a wide-awake mind, and see if your outcomes don't match those of the Master.

21

Be of Good Cheer!

How much would you pay to live your life?

Did you know that some people are so happy, they would pay anything to be able to live it exactly as it's playing itself out today?

These happy people fascinate me. When I was a professional counselor, I spent my hours with people living in many unhappy situations. The experience caused me to appreciate the simple things, such as a smile, a kind gesture, a thoughtful word of encouragement.

Not long ago I was en route to a speech, and I was hopelessly lost in the farmlands around where I live. After trying in vain to find my way, I surrendered and began looking for a local. In minutes I spied an older farmer in bib overalls cutting hay with a bushwhacker. As I pulled alongside him, he turned off his machinery and peered into my car.

"Sir, I need your help. I'm totally lost—" I began.

The farmer's eyes were as twinkly blue as any I've ever seen. He skillfully cut me off in midsentence, saying one of the kindest things I've ever heard in my life.

"Oh, you're not lost, Son. [I liked that part.] *You just took a few wrong turns*. Where do you want to go?"

Everything's gonna be all right.

He could have been nasty, abrupt, or paranoid. But for some reason he chose to cheer me up. The span of my relationship with that man took no longer than thirty seconds, yet his simple and gentle kindness will stay with me forever, I'm sure.

Jesus often did the same thing. He attempted to cheer up his followers in difficult moments. "Don't be afraid," Jesus encouraged Peter when he asked him to be a disciple. "Be of good cheer!" he called to his disciples when they freaked over seeing him walk on water. "Be happy!" he told a woman who touched his robe in order to be healed. "Your faith has made you well." To a paralyzed man, he declared, "Take heart, Son. Your sins are forgiven!" "Don't be afraid. Trust me!" he exhorted the inconsolable family of a dead girl just before he raised her. "Everything is going to be fine!"

Cheerfulness is a small matter that makes a big difference. What's most fascinating is that great leaders have a sixth sense about when some cheering is in order. If you are in a leadership position, don't be shy about an occasional spontaneous application of good cheer. Like my meeting with my thirty-second farmer friend, a small set of words, delivered with a warm smile and kind heart, can make permanent marks.

22

A View from the Top

Not many people can claim they have ruled the world. However, three have ruled everything that was known at the time they lived. The Greek Alexander the Great and the Roman Julius Caesar were the first two. The third was the king of the Franks, Charlemagne. Each of those men controlled everything in the world that was worth controlling. They answered to nobody. What's the view like from the top?

The demise of each is instructive in answering that question. Alexander the Great was partying too hard after a huge military victory and suddenly fell ill. He died within ten days. Julius Caesar was murdered by his associates.

Charlemagne was different. For all his weaknesses, he ruled well, and his subjects loved him. He died of natural causes, but when he was buried, he was placed in his sepulchre sitting upright on his throne! Get this: By his decree, his index finger was placed over a verse in a Bible beside him.

Which verse? They're the words of Jesus found in the book of Mark: "What will it profit a man if he gains the whole world, and loses his own soul?" (8:36 NKJV). That's

What would you do if you ruled the world?

a wise memorial left by someone who actually gained the whole world.

Charlemagne's perspective on power and leadership is worth thinking about. Too many of us are ambitious, driven people. Something inside makes us get up in the morning, fight our fights, win our wars, and return day after day for more. Losing perspective on what really matters is an easy trap to fall into. The view we get through the eyes of those who have been there teaches us to value something that we carry within us, yet probably value too little.

As a leader, ask yourself this question: Where is my soul? To borrow a metaphor from Jesus, if it can be found only in things that rot, decay, rust, melt, or dissolve, you've built your life on sand. Your ruin will be no less than Alexander's and Caesar's. But if your soul is founded on something timeless and true, immune from the elements of this life, then you're built on rock, as Charlemagne was. And upon that rock, you can lead a life that will never die.

23

Don't Redline Your Confidence

Ve all know fallen leaders. There are many. We can name the big ones, the high-profile people. But everyday leaders sometimes fall into traps and blow their lead in some way too. Most of them have fallen prey to the oldest scam in the book: overconfidence.

I counseled with a man who taught me a lesson in overconfidence. He had gone bust wheeling and dealing in imported gray-market cars. His stories illuminated for me the cutthroat and always risky world of borderline-legal international commerce. In his own words he admitted that he had gotten in way over his head by following a motto he had developed for himself: "I am Joe Smith. When you are Joe Smith, *you can do anything you want.*"

He followed his motto into blunder after mistake, costing him his family, his money, his career, and nearly his life. He actually told me that he lost everything except his pride. I remember staring in stunned silence when he said that. Because of pride, he nearly got his head blown off!

Jesus wrestled with overconfidence among his disciples. On many occasions, Jesus gave them authority to cast out demons, heal the sick, and proclaim his message. Heady

> *Overconfidence is the short path to self-destruction.*

stuff. It would be difficult for any of us to handle that kind of authority without sometimes looking in the mirror and smiling.

More than once, Jesus warned them not to be too cavalier about themselves and what they could do. For example, he sent them out to preach in the countryside, and they returned with news of victory and success. In sharing their excitement, Jesus said, "I have given you authority over all the power of the enemy. . . . But don't rejoice just because evil spirits obey you; rejoice because your names are registered as citizens of heaven" (Luke 10:19–20 NLT).

There is everything good about having big dreams and ignoring people who say they cannot be fulfilled. What's tricky (but essential) is balancing dreams with actuality. Keep a close watch on your self-confidence meter. Don't overrev it. Great leaders play within their own sphere of talent, knowing that creeping overconfidence can wipe them out.

24

Scar Stories

I have a copy of a painting by the Italian master Caravaggio entitled *Doubting Thomas*. It depicts Jesus with several of his disciples after his resurrection. He is lifting up his robe and showing the hole in the side of his chest where the Roman soldiers punctured him with a spear. *Thomas actually has his finger in the hole!* None of them believe it is really Jesus.

Scars generate lively conversations. Just ask people about their favorite gash, and listen. Do this: Quickly take an inventory of your body. Have you nicks and bumps? Scrapes and clefts? Crooked limbs and missing pieces? Join the club. I've often wondered if God isn't going to take us from this planet one piece at a time.

Leadership is a disfiguring business. It leaves marks occasionally on the outside, but always on the inside. Are you willing to get a scar for your cause? That willingness separates leaders from followers. Scars are part of the leadership landscape, and a willingness to endure them is part of accepting the job.

Jesus often reminded his "leaders in training" of that responsibility. At one point just before his arrest, perhaps in a moment of deep concern, he reminded them of the

---

Leaders get nicked and bruised.

suffering he was about to endure. He questioned them intensely about whether or not they thought they could handle it, for surely pain and suffering would come to them too. With hubris Peter stood and proclaimed he could endure anything. When Peter finished spouting, Jesus soberly predicted that he was fooling himself and that, in fact, Peter would deny he knew Jesus three times before sunrise.

Peter suffered deep scars from his own act of betrayal. He wept bitterly over his failure. The pain of his cowardice must have been excruciating. Yet out of that searing, burning experience evolved a man who would change the world. His wound, painful and ugly as it was, launched him on a course he could not have traveled before.

What have you learned from your scars? Have they improved you? Embittered you? Matured you? Embarrassed you? In all cases, your scars are your resources. They mark the moments you learned and prospered personally. Use the marks, and let them build within you confidence, tolerance, and depth.

25

A Players' Coach

W e have in my hometown a minor league professional hockey team. Earlier in my career as a sports performance consultant, the head coach asked me to do some motivational work with his players. What I learned from that experience taught me more about motivation than anything I gave them.

The coach was young, early thirties, and hungry. He had recently retired from professional hockey, and that evening was to be his first game of his first real coaching job. The pressure was on.

He was excited to the point of delirium about the prospects for his club. When I arrived, he escorted me around and introduced me to all his players individually as if I were his best friend. We then had a brief meeting in his office. He asked me to sit in his chair! He got me coffee! Hey, folks, *I'm a consultant*. I wasn't used to that kind of treatment. His enthusiasm did something to me, for I delivered one of the most inspired speeches of my life.

As a professional courtesy I received free tickets to the game that evening. It was classic minor league hockey with fights erupting seconds into the game. I watched as my new favorite-hockey-coach-in-the-world angrily paced

---

Be the first one to jump into the arena.

behind the bench. He was not happy with the way the game was unfolding.

When the team entered the ice for the third and final period, I noticed that the coach was missing. As the team finished skating warmup circles, one player jumped up on the bench behind the others and ripped off his helmet. It was the coach!

Now, folks, that was epic. In a flash I saw Homer, Moses, Alexander, Joan of Arc, Napoleon, and Schwarzkopf all rolled into one. His players cheered him! The fans stomped their feet. And when he entered the ice, everything changed. Everything. The papers the next day called him "a players' coach."

Jesus was a players' coach. He was always willing to strap on the skates. One of the most instructive elements of Jesus' style was that he never asked anyone to do something he had not already done many times himself. He demonstrated his style in real time; no talk, just action. At no time can we find any of his followers grumbling about his unwillingness to lead the way.

As a leader, when did you last strap on the skates? Do you have the passion and caring to try? You must press yourself into the action willfully and often. Don't expect your followers to do anything you're not doing!

26

The Glare of the Spotlight

Are you familiar with the feeling of suddenly having all eyes turn to you? It can be an awful sensation of self-consciousness and pressure. You blush with sweat, the air pulses to the beat of your spastic heart, your tongue goes thick as molasses, and spine-tingling panic swirls throughout your members. It's the glare of the spotlight, a baptism of attention awaiting all leaders. They either learn to deal with it or sweat to death.

I had an enlightening experience with this several years ago when I was asked to guest host a local CNN affiliate television station's morning talk show. The gig was for a week, and the station must have been hard up for someone to fill the spot. I agreed to do it for my expenses, which probably had much to do with my selection.

Let me tell you something: Television cameras change people. Each camera has bright red lights that glow when the camera is "live." Many strange things blitz through your brain when you see red: *Is this what Bryant Gumbel would say?* or *Did I remember to check my teeth for chives?* or *I hope nobody I know is watching this.* Despite my insecurity, I tried to put on a good show.

How will you act when all eyes are on you?

What a mistake! The producer came up to me on the first break and said some simple words that taught me a huge lesson. "Relax, Bill, and just be yourself," he said. I didn't know what he meant, but I was soon to find out.

My first guest was a very nice local singer promoting her new CD. We had lighthearted chitchat prior to her segment, and I felt very comfortable with her. Then the red light popped on, indicating we were back from a commercial break.

To my shock, she mutated right there in front of me! She stopped laughing, began to fidget, and literally became a different person. She answered my questions with wooden, rehearsed replies. I felt sorry for her because who she was when the lights were off was so much more appealing than the person who later emerged. The television audience didn't really end up knowing her.

Then it struck me: Neither did they know me. The spotlight changed *me* too.

Jesus often endured the glare. I don't think he ever thoroughly enjoyed it. Imagine having five thousand people gathered around to hear you. "Relax and be yourself" is probably the last thing you or I would think to do. Jesus responded by being open and forthcoming to a fault. His reply came from experience: not experience in *acting relaxed* in front of the world, but experience in *sharing truth from the heart*. As I can attest, doing that is not easy, but it is a goal to which we should commit ourselves.

Somewhere in your life is a spotlight, a hot spot, a pressure point, a red "on the air" light. When the heat is turned up, gain poise by being open and direct. If you catch yourself in the midst of an acting job, understand that faking it makes you look weaker than you are naturally. Your most powerful form is honest and direct, though it may not feel that way. Practice this.

27

The Discipline of Listening

One of the greatest leaders I know earned that distinction when I caught him in the act of doing something unusual. This man is the president of a small, but aggressive, financial services firm. He is a penetrating, complex character, and I'm very fond of the way he thinks and interacts with his people.

He has several insulating layers of administrative staff between himself and his employees. He really has no reason to talk with, much less fraternize with, his workers. He values remaining somewhat aloof. "Among them but not of them," I've heard him say.

But like all great leaders, he recognizes the impact of listening. One day I stopped by to see him, and his secretary told me I could find him in the telemarketers' cafeteria (his company has a well-orchestrated boiler room operation of telephone solicitors). That was the first shock. The second shock came as I rounded a corner and found him sitting on the floor *listening* to several of his solicitors describe how they would improve the place.

Imagine a multimillionaire listening to entry-level phone dialers tell him how to make his operation run better! He later told me that he learned more about improving

---

Be quiet.

his company from thirty minutes of listening on the floor than the last three books he read.

Jesus was equally practiced in the discipline of listening. It must not have always been easy to sit quietly. The disciples often asked kindergarten-level questions revolving around redundant themes. Their concerns must have seemed trite and fluffy. Yet Jesus found the patience to steadily absorb what they said. The more he listened, the more they talked. The more he listened, the closer and more resilient the bond between them grew.

Do whatever it takes today to just listen to someone. Lose the tie, let the lipstick fade, break your no-fraternizing policies, and just listen. It's the power tool of great leaders.

28

The Spirit Is Willing But . . .

V igilance. It's the fundamental fuel of self-discipline. It's the uninfringeable rule on the road to success. It's something permeating all winners. It's difficult to do on command because it requires that we override our natural tendencies. Too often only leaders can do this with any degree of reliability.

Looking objectively at the life of Jesus, we see a steadily building drama that climaxed at the cross. One of the linchpin scenes occurred late Thursday night, just prior to his betrayal and arrest. Knowing exactly what was going to happen, Jesus was in a state of agony. He brought his three best people with him to the Garden of Gethsemane that night: Peter, James, and John. After having asked them to wait while he wandered alone, he returned to find them sleeping.

Jesus couldn't believe it. "Couldn't you stay awake one hour?" he asked. "Keep alert and pray," he continued, "for though the spirit is willing, the flesh is weak." He left them and went about a stone's throw away to pray.

Returning a second time, he found them asleep again! He repeated his earlier warnings, then went away once more.

Your most difficult obstacle is yourself.

Returning a third time, he found them asleep again! "Still sleeping? Still resting?" he asked. "Up, let's be going. My betrayer is here." And with those final words began the climactic day that changed history. (See Matt. 26:36–46.)

Successful long-term leaders have self-control. In Jesus' terminology, they have mastered the flesh. They can make themselves do hard things. This aptitude sets these leaders apart from the wanna-bes.

I like the words of William Arthur Ward, who said, "We control our thoughts, or our thoughts control us. We rule our passions, or our passions rule us. We govern our habits, or our habits govern us."

Your body will rule you if you do not rule it. One of you must be in charge. Unfortunately, your body is weak. It wants comfort, warmth, and safety—often the exact things that destroy progress or effective leadership. Being in control of yourself is no more complicated than making your spirit rule. It will be one of the hardest things you ever choose to do.

29

Future Spotting

Some people possess an uncanny sense about what's going to happen. Their ability to see events unfolding like so many pieces on a chessboard amazes me.

I occasionally do an exercise in my seminars I call future spotting. Within some limits, we can all predict the future. It really isn't that hard. Consider this on two levels: First, your life is pretty well planned out if by nothing other than habit. Although you don't know exactly what will take place, say, this afternoon, you can correctly predict it in nine out of ten tries. That's pretty good future spotting.

Second, think of your life on a more immediate scale. How far into your immediate, proximate future can you predict your life perfectly? One or two or ten seconds? An hour? Knowing exactly is the hard part, but if you practice it, you'll find that you can be 99 percent accurate up to a few split seconds into the future.

Jesus often referred to Old Testament prophecy in his teaching. He would say something or do a miraculous act, then refer to the prophecy he fulfilled in doing so. But he went farther than that. He told in precise detail what was going to happen to him at the time of his crucifixion

> *Your followers need you to show them tomorrow.*

and beyond. The Jewish officials used one of his predictions to condemn him in court. ("Destroy the temple of God, and I will rebuild it in three days.")

Yet still, many people did not believe him. In all fairness believing his fantastic predictions would have been difficult. Once a group of Pharisees demanded a miraculous sign proving he was from heaven.

"You're great at looking at the sky and predicting the weather," Jesus replied, "but you can't discern the signs of the times. No sign shall be given except the sign of Jonah." (That was the second time Jesus used this reference to predict his impending crucifixion and resurrection.)

Some people are using you as a lens piece on the future. Because you are a leader, they believe you can see the future better than they can. Help them spot a glimmer of hope. How? By looking carefully at every oncoming situation and finding something to be positive about. Then, like Jesus, invite them to participate in those events with a personal challenge to act in forceful ways. Reassure your followers that they can win in all their tomorrows.

Make Something Happen

All of us carry short maxims and proverbs passed to us by our parents and guardians: "Money doesn't grow on trees"; "Are we trying to heat the neighborhood?"; "Remember to say thank you, and don't be rude"; "Do it right the first time"; that sort of thing. Do you remember a few of yours? I used to hate that I couldn't erase those things from my mind, but now I feel indebted to the elders in my life for making them irreversible.

My dad gave me a particularly indelible one. I was bored and whiny one very hot summer day. "There's nothing happenin'," I complained. He looked at me and in three short words changed my life: "Make something happen."

Nobody enjoys being corrected, but something about the simple brilliance of that comment left me, a kid, speechless. He was telling me two things: (1) I was responsible for what happened to me, and (2) I needed to change the way I thought.

Leaders make things happen. They take life where they want it to go instead of hanging on for the ride. They practice creating action. They become so accomplished, they don't know how to do anything else.

"What's happenin'" is for you to decide.

I think it's impossible for anyone with a flickering understanding of Jesus to picture him standing around with his hands in his pockets. Jesus constantly made things happen, and he encouraged his followers to do the same.

On one occasion, he sent out a group of disciples with specific instructions to spread his message. However, there was a catch: Don't take money, food, clothes, sandals, walking stick, or anything else! His directions seemed to imply that his disciples would make too many arrangements and perhaps take too little action if given reasons to dawdle. Jesus suggested they go to work and by faith let the consequences unfold. You could practically hear Jesus saying, "Just make it happen."

On another occasion, John the Baptist sent emissaries to ask Jesus if he was, in fact, the Messiah. Jesus let his actions speak for him. "Go back to John and tell him about what you have heard and seen," he said. "The blind see, the lame walk, the lepers are cured, the deaf hear, the dead are raised to life, and the Good News is being preached to the poor" (Matt. 11:4–5 NLT).

Making Jesus' leadership style happen isn't that hard. You know very well what action you must take in your life right now. You know what you've been postponing and avoiding. You know in which areas of your life you've been planning too much and acting too little. *Go forward boldly now with your work, thoughtless of the consequences or barriers*. Take action in faith, and let the consequences dictate what they will.

Headhunters

A headhunter contacted me. No, she didn't grunt and throw spears at me, or dunk me in a big black kettle of boiling water. She was very smooth on the phone. An executive recruiter, she called herself.

Headhunters have a simple job description: Find talented people, and for a fee (usually a percentage cut of first-year earnings) convince them to leave their current place of employment and join another firm. For instance, a company may be looking for someone to manage a small division. That's a huge responsibility, and you'd never find the right person with newspaper ads. Enter headhunters. These professionals get a description of what a successful executive in that position would look like, then recruiting they go! They call successful division managers in other organizations and ask for referrals, and they make countless phone calls to prospects.

The headhunter who contacted me wanted an appointment to talk to me about becoming the director of a large clinic. Being flattered and curious, I agreed.

Our meeting was brief. She entered my office (I was in private practice as a professional counselor at the time),

---

Learn to recognize teachable people.

and within about ten seconds she blurted out, "Oh, this isn't going to work!"

My curiosity intensified despite the blow to my ego. "Why not?" I asked.

"Your hair," she pointed out, "*is not gray enough.*"

I laughed at the irony, and I felt caught between feelings of gratitude and regret. I opted to apologize. "I'm sorry," I said with a chuckle.

"Oh, that's all right," she said. "Our client specifically asked that we find someone who looked professional and distinguished."

I wasn't sure how to take that. She quickly backspaced our conversation (too late!) and explained that her client was very specific about who the clinic wanted. In short, it was not me had I been Sigmund Freud incarnate!

Jesus recruited every single day of his professional life. Every interaction was devoted to finding recruits. But several items that are popular today were *absent* from his list of requirements, notably, intelligence, education, emotional stability, personal history, standardized test scores, transcripts, letters of reference, FBI background checks, urinalysis, insurability, employment history, and performance reviews.

Jesus was looking for some things that all good leaders seek in people: teachability and devotion. Cultivate and encourage these two qualities in everyone you're responsible for. These two qualities are difference makers in your ability to lead effectively.

Oh, and for the record, forget hair color.

32

Planting Seeds

A good friend of mine is a master of one of the world's complex sciences: metallurgy. He creates recipes for and oversees the production of specialized blends of metal. It's an exact science. Goof up one aspect of a batch of steel, and you get junk. It requires teamwork, for each ladleful is molten money. Errors are terribly expensive.

He has a very interesting philosophy of leadership that works exceptionally well. He says he has given up trying to understand what motivates individuals. His job, as he practices it, is not to nudge, cajole, counsel, or crucify his people. It is, rather, to set a high standard and seed everyone evenly with his expectations.

He likens it to planting seeds when you just don't know which seeds will grow and which will die. To reduce stress, he says he focuses on getting the seeds spread out as evenly as he can. Often, he has noted, seeds he is sure are spread into a barren mind sprout, and others he is sure will flourish lay fallow and dead. "You just can't know ahead of time which mind is which," he says.

You can never know exactly where your words will hit.

Jesus used a similar metaphor in describing not only his followers, but also all who hear his words. He described it like this: "A sower went out to sow. Some seeds fell by the wayside, and birds devoured them. Some fell on stony ground and sprang up fast. But the sun burned them up because they had no roots. Some fell among thorns, and when they grew up, the thorns choked them out and they produced no crop. But some fell on good ground and yielded a good crop; some thirty-, some sixty-, some a hundredfold."

Frustration over the performance of the people who follow you can destroy your confidence and effectiveness: "This is so easy and clear! Why can't they just do what I say?" Don't nurse this complaint. Play the leadership game smarter.

You'll do much better to adopt a seed planter's mentality. You cannot know how your words of direction, encouragement, admonition, or even forgiveness will sound to their ears or play out in their minds. All you can really do is commit yourself to being as clear as possible and spreading the seeds as evenly and as consistently as you can. Someone will hear. Someone will respond.

33

Power Bases

Leadership can be draining. High exposure and interpersonal intensity sap your strengths. Finding an outlet to recharge your leadership batteries is required.

I conduct a seminar entitled "Focus Your Fire." This seminar teaches one thing: how to focus all your talent, experience, energy, vision, and strength on *one thing*, whether it's one problem, one dream, one goal, or one person. Can you imagine being able to completely gather yourself in this manner for even several minutes a day?

In doing this seminar I've become concerned about how few people are actually ready for victory in their lives. I find myself telling people that they're not prepared to win because they don't know where their power base is. Sure, they vacation and rest from time to time, but they don't get *ready*. Being rested and being ready are different.

Being ready is knowing what you do well and what you do poorly, knowing where you get the best effectiveness out of yourself, and knowing how to press yourself intelligently. Getting to this point of self-understanding requires spending time alone and thinking honestly and specifically about what you want.

Find a place that renews and recharges you.

This lesson came from Jesus. He had an incandescent power base and encouraged his followers to seek it too. His biographers pointed out that he spent a great deal of time alone both early in the morning and late at night. He reported that he spent that time praying and watching God. "I can do only what I see my Father in heaven doing," he said. Whatever he did during those times alone proved highly effective for concentrating his efforts and making him a visionary leader and people mover.

A leader's mind can quickly wrap itself around new ideas. Finding a power base is one idea that, no matter how hard it may be for you to visualize, begs to be tried. Find for yourself a place that renews and refreshes you. Take time to recharge, not rest. Find your place of power, and go there often.

34

Calculating Your Net Worth

This comment may stun you: Two prominent historical leaders died thinking they had failed the world. Who were they?

Leonardo da Vinci and Thomas Jefferson.

The Italian Renaissance man da Vinci possessed one of the most fertile minds of all time. He painted, sculpted, invented, engineered, dissected, mathematized, and philosophized in a more prolific way than the world has ever seen before or since. Yet he died feeling as though his life didn't amount to much.

Thomas Jefferson helped create and single-handedly wrote the intellectual foundation for our claim to political freedom. The Declaration of Independence drew the road map by which we think about our liberties. He crafted elegant arguments and insightful treatises that inspired the formation of our nation.

Without him, our country would not be. Yet near his death, he was certain the only thing in life he had done with any degree of success was build a small dam in a creek in his backyard.

Don't "ooooh!" and "aaaah!" too much. We're just like both of them. We calculate our worth based upon a

> *You can't put your value in a ledger.*

twisted and misguided value system. We tend to be grossly unfair to ourselves, driven to measure our impact using the silliest yardstick. All we seem concerned about is what we've accomplished. This misjudgment is epidemic among leaders.

Jesus offered a refreshing perspective. He elevated the importance of quality of work, not quantity. He strongly encouraged us to lose our accounting mentality when calculating our net worth.

We see that most clearly in analyzing Jesus' blistering attack on the Pharisees, the elite temple pros of the day. The select group was obsessed with perfectly following all the rigorous temple rules. They loved their money, their possessions, and their perfection. They kept accurate records of the quantity of their goodness and gloated over the overdrafts of others.

Jesus urged something different. He pressed his followers not to be concerned about chasing all the rules to pointless perfection. Rather, he said, be kind and forgiving. Don't be obsessed with the accuracy with which you are able to follow human-devised traditions, but think of God and how you might serve him faithfully. Do good things, no matter how insignificant they seem, and don't worry about what you accomplish in the process.

35

Powerlust

We've all been bullied by people preoccupied with themselves. This can be especially infuriating if the person holds a position of authority or power. The Greek philosopher Sophocles said, "But hard as it is to learn the mind of any mortal, or the heart, till he be tried in chief authority. Power shows the man."

Successfully managing something powerful requires maturity and even-tempered judgment. This is true of power as diverse as intellect, wits, comedic ability, legal authority, talent, muscles, guns, or nuclear weapons. Only an accomplished human being can possess one of these in good measure and remain above thoughtless or crude shows of force.

Jesus had access to something quite powerful, but on two specific occasions, he showed amazing temperance in situations that would have prompted retaliation or worse in the best of us.

On one occasion, he had been treated badly in a Samaritan village. James and John, two of his most trusted and devoted followers, asked him for permission to rain down fire from heaven and destroy the town! Jesus was incredulous at their suggestion and, scolding them, said that

Be restrained and deliberate with power.

they didn't really understand what their own hearts were like. "I've come to save lives," he concluded, "not destroy them!"

The second occasion occurred as he was being arrested to be put to death. A mob arrived at the Garden of Gethsemane, and Peter, a known hothead, jumped up and sheared off the ear of the high priest's servant with a sword. Jesus rebuked him firmly.

"Put away your sword," he said. "Don't you know I could ask my Father for twelve legions of angels to protect us, and he would send them instantly?" (A single Roman legion was six thousand soldiers.) Jesus had seventy-two thousand angels at his disposal!

Where did such discretion come from? Jesus clearly stated that his intention for coming was not to glorify himself, much less to save his hide. "I have no wish to glorify myself. God wants to glorify me," he told a skeptical group of listeners. If you can, even for short periods of time, keep your attention off yourself and on the direct service of others, powerlust can be averted and life given. The power is yours to choose.

36

"If We Don't Beat Indiana . . ."

I have an acquired taste for simplicity. I love simple answers. If you seek simplicity in finding solutions to most problems, the results are worth the humility.

One of my favorite people is a successful retired businessman who freely tosses nuggets from his deep reservoir of experience. His kind smile and gentle ways make his often tough common sense easier to gulp. He consistently suggests simple ways to digest complex troubles.

I asked him outright, "What's the secret of success?" He has been successful by all means of human measure, so I hung on his answer.

"I heard Woody Hayes interviewed once," he began. (Woody Hayes was the head football coach at Ohio State University and one of the winningest coaches in college football history.) "The interviewer asked him about the game against his arch rival Michigan, still several weeks away. Woody looked at the interviewer and, in his inimitable style, said, 'If we don't beat Indiana this week, Michigan doesn't matter.'

"That's the secret of my success," my friend said matter-of-factly. "I made a commitment that I'd deal with one problem, one person, one situation at a time, because unless

---

Put all your attention on the next thing.

you can get through each in its order, what happens tomorrow doesn't matter. I put all my attention on the next thing I had to deal with, and I never stopped until I was here."

I couldn't help feeling a little upbraided by his suggestion. Many of us know the trap of becoming panicky as the problems swarm in on us. Not seeing an exit or end to the morass, we quickly lose hope, the first step toward disaster.

Masterful leaders understand staying focused on just the next thing. Jesus spoke of that often. He encouraged his followers to pray for their daily bread and not worry about what God would do with them tomorrow. "Today has enough troubles of its own," he said. He focused his disciples not on meals, clothing, or conveniences, but on faith in dealing with the people God placed in their path that day. Jesus intuitively knew that his mission was to attend to the realities of people today, not the mysteries of tomorrow.

That's advice any of us can follow. Take ten seconds sometime today, and focus yourself completely on the next person, project, or priority you encounter. Leadership begins when an individual makes a committed effort in something specific and immediate.

37

Pass the Grenades

I was speaking before a group of single parents. A woman stood and asked me a hard question. To her credit, she warned me that she was "passing me a grenade." I responded that I usually handled only little bombs and let my wife, Kathi, handle the big ones! She told me that it would make just a teeny little boom and that I shouldn't be afraid. Emboldened, I answered her question with fearless authority. Kathi would have been proud.

When passed a grenade of heavy responsibility, people do one of four things:

1. They ignore it. This response happens often inside homes and families.

2. They blame others for not dealing with the responsibility. This happens in jobs where rigid hierarchy makes people think in "it's not my job" terms.

3. They make excuses: "I never handled a situation like this before"; "I might get in trouble"; or "What if something goes wrong?"

4. They assume it. "It's my responsibility. Let me deal with it."

Jesus was a dragnet for responsibility. He was proactive in spotting problems before they arrived and dealing

Seize responsibility.

with them personally. As all good leaders do, he was effective in reminding others of their responsibilities and calling them to attack with zeal. Ignoring, blaming, and excuse making were not part of his style.

Today, find a grenade, and deal with it before it blows. Perhaps it's a relationship you've ignored because it's simmering in bad feelings. Perhaps it's a problem you think belongs to someone else. Maybe it's a problem you've been excusing yourself from handling. An easy way to take leadership today is to seek more responsibility. Be the person willing to step forward and risk what awaits you there.

38

On-the-Job Training

Several years ago I was briefly involved in a real estate venture with two partners. I have to struggle to find words appropriate to describe my experience. The problem was not the buildings; the problem was me.

Having no experience as an absentee landlord, I had to be baptized in the truth. I thought being a real estate tycoon was as simple as buying up multifamily homes, putting ads in the paper for tenants, filling the vacancies, and watching my bank accounts swell. On paper the beauty of the system was breathtaking.

My on-the-job training revealed my foolishness. Since my partners were involved in other ventures and gone most of the time, I agreed to assume responsibility for daily upkeep and repair of the properties. I quickly discovered you can't have $75-per-hour craftsmen going to your properties every day to fix things. I learned to plumb, plaster, wire, and fix broken windows by reading books and making many costly errors. I had nobody I could ask for help, so I made it up as I went. The reality of being a real estate baron was far different from my visions.

The whole experience was a sad debacle that I finally escaped, but not before it had completely wrapped its tentacles of trouble all around me.

Put down the manuals and lead.

Did Jesus feel those tentacles of trouble with his disciples? He faced many difficult training challenges. He taught them all on the job with no manuals, no official work hours, and no tight supervision. What's more, his trainees were not the Wharton-caliber, goal-directed, self-starting executive types you'd expect. They were for the most part common people of the day. Add to this the fact that his teachings weren't intellectual Twinkies and you can understand why his followers were often confused.

Yes, Jesus knew all about tentacles.

But Jesus succeeded in building the group into leaders. How? Jesus trusted his little band of rabble and encouraged them constantly. On several occasions, he specifically empowered them to cast out demons, heal the sick, and preach. Were they qualified, certified, and capable of handling those rather powerful things? Not at first. But knowing that mistakes would be common, Jesus patiently guided them. He corrected their thinking when they needed it and let them feel the power he put at their disposal.

To lead better today, don't constantly look to manuals or mentors. What you've already experienced in your world qualifies you to step forward with some authority. On your job today, you already have more experience and authority than any of the twelve disciples had. And they changed the world. If you don't know enough to lead by now, you'll probably never know enough. Think about that, then lead on.

☙ 39 ☙

Burn the Ships

Hernando Cortés. If you missed that day of high school history, let me catch you up. Cortés is remembered as the Spaniard who captured Mexico for his king. But he is also known in history for a galvanizing act of leadership he performed on the coast of the Gulf of Mexico.

Cortés led a band of about six hundred men to the coast of Mexico with the underwriting support of the governor of Cuba. But being loyal to the king in Spain, Cortés felt the land should be claimed for Spain, not his Cuban benefactor. Cortés sensed dissension among his men, and he heard rumors that they would mutiny and sail back to Cuba. In a dramatic effort to save the expedition he had all the ships burned. Nobody was leaving Mexico. The men had no choice but to fight by his side or die.

Good leaders have at their disposal various means to gain commitment from followers. Good leaders know that nothing can happen without a passionate and fully devoted crew. Fortunately for most of us, nobody can force us onto the beaches of a foreign land and burn our means of escape (though some leaders and bosses would like to try!).

The path to greatness opens to people with no way out.

Rather, they must coax us to give more of ourselves, to commit our best.

Jesus was no different. It's worth repeating that not one of his followers was being forced or threatened. They were by his side willingly. If Jesus did anything, it was to check and recheck their commitment. He didn't want to burn the ships to keep them. He knew he couldn't force people into the commitment they were going to need. He wanted them to voluntarily burn the ships. He wanted them to be self-committed.

How can we create ship-burning leadership? It took Jesus three years of constant attention and challenge to create that sort of following. Even then, many people did abandon him, not wanting any part of a crew destined for martyrdom. Yet he foretold the nearness of the long-ago-prophesied kingdom, and he encouraged his followers to persist in their strange land despite bleak prospects.

Sometimes good leadership boils down to nothing more than being the one willing to ask the hard questions. Today, ask your crew members a hard, burning question: "How committed are you?"

40

Think Globally

Anybody who has spent time on the Internet now understands what "thinking globally" means. In the past several years, I've developed friendships and associations around the world, all from the comfort of my recliner and the efforts of my globe-trotting laptop. For years large businesses and others have been thinking globally, but only recently has the world become literally close to everyone. At this moment, almost anyone on the face of the earth is a mere key flick away from you.

One of the very last instructions Jesus left for his disciples had to do with marketing. "Go into all the world and proclaim the good news," he said. Two thousand years ago Jesus was thinking globally.

What's important to note from a leadership perspective is that the success of his marketing plan was phenomenal, especially for the times. Within several short years, congregations of believers had sprung up all over the major capitals of the Roman Empire (despite death threats to those who professed publicly) and even as far away as Rome itself.

It all began on the shores of the Sea of Galilee when Jesus challenged his followers to talk to others about what

Feel free to develop a bigger vision.

they had seen. Sometimes the most important leadership activity is to talk about what you've witnessed. The disciples demonstrated the power of simple sharing.

There is really no need to ask anyone's advice on how to do this: *Advice is often what you ask for when you already know what you have to do.* Form a clear statement of the message you want to spread, then start talking.

41

Lessons from a Grand National Stock Car

A Grand National stock car rolling down the track at more than two hundred miles per hour seems like a mighty strange place to get a lesson on leadership. To be honest, it is a strange place. As a professional sports consultant, I worked often with race car drivers and had the chance to view their world up close and personal. A driver's world is noisy, dirty, exhausting, tense, dreadful at times, and always seesawing on the brink of disaster. Not exactly your quiet Sunday afternoon spin.

The cars are lightweight and precise, awesomely overpowered and beautifully adorned. On the track they purr smooth and true through the turns, then growl into eight-hundred-horsepower beasts on the straights. They're aerodynamically perfect, except for one thing. They have one feature the engineers cannot eliminate.

At top speeds the cars create a strong air current behind them called a draft. On the straightaways they basically become multimillion-dollar vacuum cleaners, sucking along any car that snuggles up close behind. It's somewhat

> *Decide where you're going, and others will get behind you.*

like following an eighteen-wheeler closely on the interstate. By steering into the river of pulling air, other race car drivers can follow along behind the leader, conserving precious fuel and reducing wear and tear on their cars. The draft behind the lead car is a good place to follow.

Metaphorically speaking, Jesus had a strong interpersonal draft. I'm certain that on more than one occasion, he looked around and was astounded by the numbers of people nearby. His disciples trailed him closely, pulled along, it would seem, by the powerful draft of his mission and intensity. And Jesus didn't mind a bit.

I've found you can effectively simulate this kind of "people draft" by getting in a hurry and getting more serious about reaching a goal. Something about the intensity of a person consumed by a direction creates a pull that followers find intriguing. The writer Basil King said, "Be bold, and mighty forces will come to your aid." Don't be surprised if you turn around and suddenly find people following you. It means you're being a leader.

~ 42 ~

Add a Little Pizzazz

We're preprogrammed to a fault. Most of us have only one or two ways of doing every single activity in our lives. Our precision has led us down a road of blandness and boredom.

Think of something routine such as taking a shower. If you're like me, you've done it about the same way since you were very young: Start at the top and work your way down. I don't vary much from the overall pattern, and I do it with thoughtless accuracy day after day.

It's the same with smaller behaviors such as washing your hands, answering the phone, making coffee, sneezing in public, waving good-bye, and so on. By creating habits, you've subtly robbed yourself of some originality, and the older you get, the more difficult it is to try new things. Adding a little pizzazz to your routines unlocks life and changes people around you.

Let me give you a real-life example to try. Most of us have only one way of shaking hands with people. However you reach, grip, squeeze, shake, and release is pretty well identical time after time. Shake hands with someone now (or before the end of the day), and notice how you do it.

Your flexibility opens new opportunities.

Now, add pizzazz: Shake hands differently. For example, shake with the wrong hand, squeeze the other person's hand gently, or clamp down ferociously. Maybe shake it around wildly like a rattlesnake has chomped on the end of your finger! Just do something different. If you succeed, congrats. You now have two ways to shake hands.

Jesus was a very personal leader. He intuitively knew that some people needed to be pushed, and others needed to be pulled. He was skilled in doing both. He was not afraid to be the most visible and flexible source of pizzazz if it meant getting to just one person and unfreezing him or her. His oftentimes unorthodox behavior was always oriented toward his mission, never toward personal gain.

He gave all people a daily dose of pizzazz for the purpose of educating and encouraging them.

43

Jerk Radar

In my profession I frequently interact with secretaries and executive assistants at various levels. These gatekeepers are expert and tireless in shielding their bosses. One day I overheard a gatekeeper in action. She politely, but firmly, pancaked an unprepared solicitor.

I asked her the secret for deciding who gets through and who doesn't. She confided to me that she uses "jerk radar." Naturally, I asked the same question you're asking, "What's 'jerk radar'?"

"It's knowing the difference between persuasiveness and credibility," she said. "If someone is just persuasive, you can hear it in his voice. It's an instant turnoff. You can hear credibility in voices too. If a stranger is credible, she is much more likely to get through."

She went on to describe many more interesting aspects of the pit bull business, but one lesson really hit home: Strangers can see through you more easily than you might think. Actually, we can all see through one another pretty well. We're all competent fakes, and we know it. In order not to be taken in by someone better than we are, our jerk radar is at work most of the time.

Many followers are suspicious by nature.

So how do you effectively lead people while they're scanning you with their jerk radar? Lead as Jesus led.

Jesus must have been something special. He had the curious and compelling qualities of being believable *and* credible. On one occasion, Jesus had just finished preaching, and as usual, the crowds were stunned. An eyewitness made a simple, yet profound, observation about his preaching that summarized what I think was a huge part of Jesus' success: "He taught them as one having authority, and not as the scribes" (Mark 1:22 NKJV).

You can learn this sort of leadership. Rarely does the Bible say that Jesus "led" anyone. However, it cites several instances when Jesus "brought" people to places. That may seem like a minor point, but it's not, especially where jerk radar is activated. Leadership in the form of a personal accompaniment creates a powerful sense of allegiance. "Do what I say" leadership tactics may create only resistance.

Be a person who brings people to places. Be they friends, family, customers, or clients, adopting an escort attitude ushers people to a certain way of thinking that puts you in a firmer leadership role. Don't get caught being a jerk, coercing, conniving, lying, and yelling at people to follow you. Get next to them, and walk with them.

44

Veritas Plateat

A Latin phrase I keep near my desk guides everything I write:

Veritas Plateat;
Veritas Placeat;
Veritas Moveat.

Translated, that means, "Make it plain; make it simple; make it moving."

Leadership is a hot topic these days. For many reasons we have become concerned with the mechanics of developing better leadership and bringing along new talent. It's easy to think that something as important as leadership should be complicated. It's not.

I am reminded of the sage advice I received from a mentor in graduate school. When I asked what I needed to do to be a great thinker, he said plainly, "Think every day." When I asked what I needed to do to be a great counselor, he said, "Counsel every day." When I asked him how I could become a great writer, he said, "Write every day." Had I asked him how to be a great leader, he would have said, "Lead every day."

Is your leadership clear, simple, and moving?

So simple.

Jesus was *plateat, placeat,* and *moveat.* He laid out his message as plainly as he was able. His words were so simple that even children could understand. They were so moving that they still move people. Jesus literally never spoke about leadership. He always spoke about such things as forgiveness and love, mercy and kindness. His values epitomized simplicity.

Being a leader of this variety is probably much easier than you think. His message is not confusing, and if you feel lost, you're thinking too hard. Throttle your thinking back, and try to perceive Jesus' style of leadership from the innocent perspective of a child. Things look much simpler from that vantage point.

45

Be Patient

*L*eadership is what I call a glow word. It leaps off the page with an identity all its own. The word associations we make with it are vivid (*strength, vision, power, authority*, etc.). And its connotations are clear. *Leadership* has panache that we create in our heads and assign to people exercising the title.

Patience is not one of the first descriptors that jump to mind. Patience is not a virtue we routinely associate with leaders. I believe we hold a collective opinion that patient, nice, gentle, people are naive or stupid. Though we judge them to be very kind, we also think of them as perhaps a bit uninformed, gullible, and perhaps even lazy. As a result of this mind-set, many leaders feel pressure to be impatient and perhaps pushy. "That's what good leaders do," goes the reasoning.

That was not what Jesus decided. Remember that Jesus led inside an unusual context. The religious authorities and teachers of the day were strict, demanding, and no-nonsense people. Their style of leadership was top-down and power driven. The Roman legal authorities were

> *Most followers haven't had the pleasure of following a patient leader.*

vicious and cruel. The commoners of the day were used to their leaders being nasty, bitter, and unbending.

Into that picture stepped Jesus. He was kind, informed, savvy, gentle, and . . . well, nice. To the discouraged, downtrodden, abused, cowering people of the day, he must have seemed out of place. Quite different from the unfriendly teachers, prophets, and authorities they were used to dealing with.

A marvelous example of his fine-tuned application of gentleness and innocence occurred when he selected Nathanael to be a disciple. "Behold, an Israelite indeed, in whom is no deceit!" he observed (John 1:47 NKJV).

People warmed to Jesus quickly, and he to them.

But the changeover wasn't easy. Jesus needed to inspire boldness, kindness, mercy, and love in a people who had all those qualities whipped out of them. He needed patience and long-range vision.

Sometimes the greatest leadership you can provide is to wait steadfastly for people to catch up. Be patient, and let gentleness be your guide. Don't scream and yell, but softly say over and over again, "Come *this* way." It is what we might call *classic Jesus*.

46

Play

Strong-willed and determined people can be joyless, absorbed, and driven like a machine. We've all worked for a few. There is no excitement in these people that has any possibility of filtering down to inspire followers. Count on your flock to consistently buck blind duty.

Great leaders know how to play. It's such a fun word, *play*. Play has awesome revival value. It has been said by no less than Freud himself that the definition of good mental health is the ability to work and play, presumably in equal measure.

Jesus seemed to understand play. He knew how to relax and enjoy occasional respites. He attended wedding parties, feasts, celebrations, holiday retreats, and dinner engagements. People must've felt a great deal of comfort with him in these situations. He was always a welcomed, if not honored, guest.

On one occasion, he was having dinner with some known thugs and must've been having too much fun. The Pharisees (grumpy workaholics if there ever were any) saw him there, no doubt fueling their opinion of him as a drunk and a lazy glutton. In response to their tongue-lashing he warned them that what God wanted was not solemn duty

Make room for mirth, fun, and play.

to the letter of their law, but mercy and kindness. Jesus seemed to be saying, "Lighten up and be nice to these folks."

Can you play? Do you know how to take a giant step back from your duties to laugh hard, sweat for pleasure, and appreciate a sunset, good music, or a child's chuckle? Can you make and keep friends and play furiously with them? What's easy for us all is to be consumed by our duty. What's hard is letting it all go for the purpose of play.

47

Avoid Legal Entanglements

Our country is litigation crazy. There are many reasons for this, and the problem isn't going away soon. You wouldn't think civilized, educated, reasonable people would pursue some of the complaints we read about daily, but they do. Legal action is costing everyone lots of money and wasting lots of precious time.

Good leaders seem to have a sixth sense about using time wisely. They just seem to know what's productive to them and what's frivolous. Very rarely will you find a leader who wants anything to do with legal adventures. Some of the best advice I ever received was "avoid legal entanglements."

You might be surprised that Jesus was a proponent of that philosophy. On one occasion, he told his listeners this: "Judge for yourself what is right! Try hard to reconcile with your enemy before you get to court, lest you lose and have to go to jail." He repeatedly encouraged his followers to be humble, direct, and forgiving with both debtors and debtees. In short, be a peacemaker, not a war maker.

It's a good way for leaders to think. Encourage the people under the umbrella of your leadership to try hard to

Avoid the court system.

work things out among themselves. Avoid punching the attorney button. Act as if legal options aren't available, even though in some cases they're the only remedy. Do what you can to encourage those around you to gain a measure of humility, forgiveness, and direct problem solving. It's a mind-set in which everyone wins BIG.

48

If I Could Have Only
One Quality

If you could have only one leadership quality, what would it be?

Pharaoh said more worship from his subjects.
Nebuchadnezzar said wealth.
Aristotle said intelligence.
Julius Caesar said power.
Adolf Hitler said world respect.
Machiavelli said political savvy.
King Solomon said wisdom.
Alexander the Great said more land.
Thomas Jefferson said independence.
Susan B. Anthony said suffrage.
Frederick Douglass said freedom.
Abe Lincoln said unity.
Albert Schweitzer said respect for life.
FDR said fearlessness.
Winston Churchill said tenacity.
Buddha said karma.

If you could add only one leadership quality to yourself, what would it be?

Muhammad said sovereign allegiance.
John Stuart Mill said knowledge.
Ben Franklin said insight.
Gandhi said self-discipline.
Emperor Hirohito said world domination.
Albert Einstein said peace.
The pope said piety.

I cannot say for sure what Jesus would have said if posed that question directly. He spoke often about faith, and he repeatedly urged his disciples to have more. Hope was a constant theme as well. Of course, love and mercy were always near his lips.

The nearest we see Jesus answering this hypothetical question was when someone asked which of the Ten Commandments was most important. "'Love the Lord with all your heart, soul, and mind,' and 'Love your neighbor as yourself,'" he replied.

I believe that I would choose the ability to more fully believe everything that Jesus said. In short, faith.

As a leader, what would you choose?

49

Thanklessness

M y wife, Kathi, works in the public school system. She is one of the leaders who move about quietly making things happen. Several years ago she and a group of other teachers wrote a grant proposal seeking money to do special education work with needy kids. They received the grant, and they conducted a wildly successful program to improve the language and social skills of kids who might not ever have the means to get that sort of training.

Their efforts received no thanks. Nobody in the community mentioned what they had done. The school board didn't recognize them. Their colleagues didn't cheer them. The kids' parents didn't call them.

Leadership can be a thankless position.

Jesus knew all about this. On one occasion, Jesus healed ten lepers. They were standing at a distance, crying out for Jesus' attention. He looked at them and said, "Go, show yourselves to the priests." And as they went, their leprosy disappeared.

One of the men, a hated Samaritan, noticed that he was healed and raced back to find Jesus. When he found Jesus, he fell at his feet, saying, "Thank God, I am healed!"

Learn to say, "Thank you."

Jesus asked, "Didn't I heal ten of you? Where are the other nine?" Knowing the answer, he looked at the cleansed man and said, "Stand up and go. Your faith has made you well."

I suppose a 10 percent thankfulness rate is about average. Adjust yourself to it, and in Jesus' words, keep doing what you are assigned to do, even when people are thankless.

You might want to take all of this a step farther. Take it upon yourself to thank the leaders in your life. Thank them specifically for what they have meant to you. It may be a little embarrassing, but be assured they haven't been thanked in a while.

50

Second Thoughts

Many good potential leaders disqualify themselves from leadership roles on the basis of occasional self-doubts. If they only knew the real story. I've counseled and consulted with many leaders who outwardly never give a hint of self-doubt or second-guessing, yet they privately doubt themselves often.

I've come to believe an ironclad rule you can rely on as surely as the sun rising in the east: Even the strongest people wonder at times about themselves and their plans. Second-guessing is part of the leadership mix.

Have you ever been in anguish so intense you began sweating blood? Most of us haven't. It's a tangible sign that someone is facing something immediate and horrid. The Bible says Jesus felt that kind of agony in his final hours as a free man. At the time Jesus was alone in a garden overlooking Jerusalem. He prayed that if possible, God would not make him endure what was coming his way. "But," Jesus concluded, *"your* will be done."

Do you know what he did then? It was classic great leadership. He boldly faced the angry mob. He lunged forward in faith. Good or bad, he knew his life was firmly in

---

Wondering whether you're doing the right thing is perfectly normal.

the palm of God's hand. He understood his role and purpose, and his commitment to completing the mission was unqualified.

Great leaders realize their shortcomings. It's good leadership to keep one eye on our soft spots while forging ahead. It's wise to have second thoughts. But should you cower in the face of challenges to your decisions? Of course not. Rather, courageously and forcefully look with steely reality at yourself and the leadership you provide.

In the face of the second doubts that will surely come to you, go forward anyway. Take care not to be paralyzed or muted by fears and second-guessing that I assure you are coming toward you now.

51

The Cost of Leadership

Does the saying go "you get what you pay for" or "you pay for what you get"? Good leaders know they're both true.

Being a leader can be personally expensive. Few of us can relate to being on the cutting edge of something. The leading edge exacts a toll. It takes something away from the few souls who hang themselves out there. It's not as romantic as we may be seduced into believing.

What are some of these expenses? Misunderstanding, *loneliness,* alienation, *loneliness,* forfeiting certain friends, *loneliness,* desertion of key supporters, and *loneliness.* No, there is no typo: Loneliness is ever present. Are you curious to feel what it's like to be really alone? It's easy to generate: Spend an hour doing what Jesus did.

Jesus was way ahead of the curve on the loneliness situation. He was not dependent on the praise and approval of others, and he encouraged his followers to learn independence for themselves. It was a good thing too. Leadership in the life-change arena would be solitary. He desperately wanted to root out the people with a loneliness allergy.

Get prepared to go it alone.

Unfortunately, his disciples never seemed to take seriously his warning that soon he would be gone and they'd be on their own. They were more intoxicated with immediate personal priorities, such as being the Master's favorite follower, securing reservations for the best seats next to the throne of God, and playing bodyguard and keeping "lesser" followers at bay. I am thankful, however, that for all their lack of enlightenment when Jesus was here, they did a remarkable job of carrying on alone after his resurrection.

At one point, Jesus said, "I send you out as sheep in the midst of wolves. Therefore be wise as serpents and harmless as doves" (Matt. 10:16 NKJV). This is great leadership advice. Don't let the loneliness of your leadership position pain you too badly. We're all alone in this . . . together.

❧ 52 ❧

Quitting

I've run several marathons. To say I enjoyed them would be untrue. I learned a lot, though. The hardest part of running one of those things is the training. It takes a long time to prepare (four months in my case), it makes your feet sore, it bites hours out of each day, and it's boring. Unless you're in better shape than I am or really have a masochistic streak, you regularly think of quitting.

In the endless boredom of running mile after mile, I've developed an interesting little reason why quitting is bad. It's not a major esoteric truth. It's just a practical insight: You shouldn't quit because *it makes quitting the next time too easy*. Quitting sets a mental precedent, making it easy to stop again if you get the slightest pain. It's a mentality you can't afford if you want to compete well.

On one occasion, Jesus was so exasperated that he sounded tremblingly close to quitting. He happened to drop in on a debate between some religious officials and several of his disciples over the healing of a young boy. The disciples had been given authority to do that sort of thing, but for lack of faith, they failed. The ever-present critics were probably taunting them for it.

Quitting now makes it easy to quit later.

As Jesus approached the fracas, people came running to watch. At the center of the fray was the boy's father, who begged Jesus to heal his son. In the midst of the confusing and compromising moment, Jesus fumed aloud: "You faithless generation, how long will I have to be with you before you believe? Bring the boy to me." With Jesus' quick rebuke the afflicting demon departed, leaving the boy so still that those in the crowd thought he was dead.

I can see Jesus rolling his eyes in frustration as he lifted the kid to his feet. His momentary exasperation gave way to more warmth and tenacity. Jesus never quit. That was the way he played the leadership game.

No matter how desperate you feel, press on. Sometimes assistants, partners, coworkers, and others will disappoint you in the most grating and infuriating ways. You may even blow your cool a bit and say words that you didn't intend to say. But don't quit. If Jesus tells us anything, it's to maintain hope and not quit.

53

The 50/20 Rule

Hardly a person lives who hasn't heard the maxim "If the world gives you lemons, make lemonade." It's cute and provides occasional refreshment to people roasting in one of life's inevitable deserts. However, its real value lies in being able to force a new way of thinking about our problems. It makes us think radically.

There have been many variations on this theme over time. It originated in the Bible from a distant relative of Jesus. Being the history buff he was, Jesus was probably influenced by his great-uncle (thirty-nine generations removed) Joseph, son of Jesus' great-grandfather (forty generations removed) Jacob. Their story is well worth retelling.

Joseph was the much-favored baby boy of Jacob. The other brothers couldn't stand little Joey and secretly sold him into slavery. Jacob was crushed when his conniving sons came with the story that little Joseph had been killed by a wild animal. Through an epic sequence of destiny, Joseph ended up in Egypt interpreting dreams for the royal family of Pharaoh. He was so good that he predicted a drought and averted a disaster for the country. That made Joseph popular and influential.

Start expecting a miracle.

In the midst of the drought, Joseph's brothers traveled to Egypt, knowing that was their best hope of finding food. When they were ushered into the presence of Joseph, they didn't recognize their long-since-forgotten little brother. But Joseph recognized them, and he was able to reconcile with them and see his father before he died.

The climactic reunion is found in Genesis 50:20. Reminding his egg-faced brothers about their little sales escapade, Joseph said, "What you intended for evil, God turned into something good."

Genesis 50:20: the 50/20 rule.

Start looking at problems with new eyes. Instead of giving in to the anguish of a life glitch, intently search for how you can use your terrible scenario *as the pivotal event in a great scenario*. This is no ideology; it's an act of faith, and that faith grows peculiarly vital with practice. Should you be surprised that Jesus promised that would happen if you'd only believe?

Take an index card, and write down a big problem you face today. Then look with expectation at how that problem will be the critical event that leads on to something wonderful. The 50/20 rule works, but you must provide the climate of faith for it to reveal itself.

54

Butch and Sundance

The story of bank robbers Butch Cassidy and the Sundance Kid was brought to life on the big screen in the early 1970s. Most of the movie wasn't historically accurate, but it had great entertainment value.

One of the few segments of the movie that was true was the finale. Butch and Sundance were American outlaws on the run from the law, holed up in a desolate ranch in Bolivia with what seemed like the entire Bolivian army surrounding the place. The army had "dead or alive" orders, so their rifles were fixed, ready to eliminate the troublesome *pistoleros*.

Both Butch and Sundance were badly wounded from a previous gunfight. Not knowing the size of the militia awaiting quietly outside, they thought they could shoot their way out of the mess to safety. Girding themselves with what ammo they had available and mustering all their courage, they broke out through the front door in a dead run. Literally. The memorable scene was that final burst, frozen in time as the sound track boomed to life with the thunder of hundreds of guns firing volley after volley at the doomed pair. The picture turned black-and-white, then faded to black.

Keep firing.

Jesus was completely doomed from the start. It was a destiny he was prepared to accept. There were many moments when, like Butch and Sundance, he was literally under siege for his life. But that was where the likeness ended. Jesus knew clearly when, where, and why he would be eliminated. Enduring the anguish of knowing how his life would end, he foretold it many times. I suppose the only thing that kept him going was that he saw the whole picture, and clearly knew that his death was only the beginning.

We all have our Bolivian showdowns. Take a quick glance at this list of problems that can beset a modern home or business:

- Critical material shortages
- Intractable relationship problems
- Labor unrest
- Cash flow worries
- Customer dissatisfaction
- Lean and hungry competition
- Downsizing
- Hiring and firing
- Management disarray
- Miscommunication
- Sour partnerships
- Debt
- Managing immature people
- Envy
- Cutting corners
- Chapter 11 bankruptcy

Come out firing. In spite of steep odds Jesus never quit. I once heard the actor Anthony Newley quoted as saying, "A big shot is just a little shot that kept on shooting." Jesus' style of leadership under conditions of adversity and hatred was a living example. No matter how bad it gets, keep firing.

55

Is That All There Is?

Not long ago I was attending a Young Presidents Organization meeting as a guest. The YPO is a group of corporate presidents, mostly younger, with real talent, energy, competitiveness, and brio in their ranks. All these people are leaders who have been quite successful.

That's why I was hammered by the presentation that evening. A dynamic young guy stood up and asked for quiet. Then in dramatic fashion, he began reading the lines from Peggy Lee's famous song "Is That All There Is?" It's a whimsical retrospective of things in life that are supposed to be a big deal but, after lots of hype, end up being no big deal at all.

> *Is that all there is?*
> *Is that all there is?*
> *If that's all there is, my friend,*
> *then let's keep on dancing. . . .*

At the end of the reading, the room was silent. For a brief moment all those successful, influential, strategically connected, well-heeled people were wondering if, after the climb to the pinnacle of their world, that was all there was.

There's always more than meets the eye.

It was a heavy, palpably uncomfortable moment with hard questions hanging in the air.

Jesus' disciples thought they were on the cutting edge of a kingdom that would last forever. In spite of Jesus' repeated teachings and warnings that it wasn't what they thought, they persisted in erroneous and incomplete understanding. Either they were not listening, or they didn't want to believe what they were taught.

Can't you just hear them, standing in the crowds near the cross, three years of their lives committed to a man now hanging lifeless, asking themselves, "Is this all there is?" The reality must have been emotionally ripping.

A master stroke of Jesus' leadership genius was a steady insistence that "this" is not all there is. In fact, a large part of his leadership and teaching oriented listeners to the future. He wanted people obsessed not so much with short-term problems but with long-range vision. In almost every single interaction he had, he seemed to be saying, "There is so much more than what's here. Look!" If you think he was kidding, read what his disciples did after Jesus left the scene.

The same holds true with your life. There is always much more to happiness and satisfaction than meets the eye. But it takes leadership to see it, courage to mine it, and faith to make it come to life. Be the person who spearheads that effort today.

56

Back to the Basics

In leading and managing any enterprise, a leader recognizes that simple problems may cause the greatest trouble. Simple things such as misunderstanding, misreading one another's motives, not knowing the goal, not getting helpful input or feedback from key team members, and so on. It's the job of a good leader to take followers back to the basics frequently and review the simple rules that make complex operations work well.

Jesus often took his followers back to the basics. The most stunning example was at an impromptu breakfast meeting with several of his disciples. The meeting took place in the quiet aftermath of his crucifixion and resurrection. Most of his staff had scattered after his death. All those people, so loyal and brave, fled like rats as the debacle unfolded.

Jesus caught up with them several days after his resurrection. He was waiting on the shore of the Sea of Galilee at dawn one morning when they arrived from a fishing expedition. He had breakfast cooking over a charcoal fire. The men were scared to death to ask him anything. We can easily imagine why.

> *Regularly bring your followers*
> *back to the basics.*

Rather than scold, humiliate, or berate those guys, Jesus took them back to the basics. While they were eating, Jesus turned to Peter and asked, "Do you love me?"

"Of course I do," Peter replied.

"Then feed my sheep," said Jesus.

Pretty basic. Jesus called him back to that basic question three times in all, each time reminding Peter of his simple mission: Follow Jesus and feed his sheep.

At the inevitable moments when your leadership is challenged, your direction questioned, your means attacked, your motivations doubted, take your followers back to the basics, whatever they are. If you don't know what your basics are, begin the task of finding out. It may be one of the most vital leadership moves you'll ever make.

The Blondin Challenge

I am a student of people, preoccupied with our unique human abilities, flaws, potentials, and mistakes. We're all full of surprises. Just about the time you think you've got somebody figured out, WHAM! The person does something that bewilders your logic.

I am most obsessed with discovering the range of our talents. How far can we push ourselves? The answer to that question lies not in principle, but in experience. Some people try pushing their talents as far as they'll reach. These are heroic folks, and we depend on them. As Bernard Malamud said, "Without heroes, we are all plain people and don't know how far we can go." The stories of those who have pushed themselves to incredible levels are awe inspiring. Yet the feats of the few renew vigor and dreams for all of us; they redefine the quality of life.

Blondin, the French aerialist, was one of the finest tightrope walkers of all time. He is best known as the one who walked a wire over Niagara Falls. On that crossing, crowds of people watched in breathless terror as he maneuvered across the wire and back again. Finally, he returned to the American side to throngs of cheering fans and media.

Hop on!

"You are the greatest, Blondin. You can do anything. Nobody in the world is as good as you!" they cried.

When the cheering subsided, Blondin thanked the people, then offered a challenge. "You think I'm wonderful?" he teased.

"Yes! You are the greatest!" they cheered.

"Well, good," he is reported to have said. "Then I should have no trouble getting a volunteer for my next act!" he said. "I need someone to ride atop my shoulders as I cross back over the falls one more time."

The crowd fell silent.

"Just one," he repeated.

After a long pause, one lone man stepped forward and climbed onto Blondin's shoulders. He and the man headed back across the wire.

Forty-five minutes later, both returned, having entertained the crowds while writing their names in the history books of great talent and great faith.

Jesus challenged his followers to do one thing: Trust him enough to climb onto his shoulders. Being a follower of Jesus was actually easy after the first step, but it required some faith and some effort. Since Jesus didn't order anyone around, his followers were responsible for their own choices. He never ordered them to clamber aboard. He challenged them to join him for the ride of a lifetime.

Challenge the people in your spheres of life to share your sense of faith and possibility. Challenge them to climb aboard, to follow you where you're going and in the adventure you've chosen to pursue.

⌒ 58 ⌒

One More Move

A story is told of former world chess champion Bobby Fischer when he was a young boy. His mother took him to a museum, and he happened upon a painting that caught his eye. It depicted a bedraggled, exhausted older man slumped over a chessboard. Few of his pieces were left on the board, and he was conceding the game. On the other side of the board was his fresh and snappy opponent, Satan. The painting was entitled *Checkmate*.

Already a chess prodigy, young Bobby Fischer stood looking at the painting for a long time. His mother soon tired of it and moved around the remainder of the gallery, finally returning to find Bobby still entranced by that painting. "Come now, Bobby, we have to go."

Bobby Fischer did not stop staring, thinking. One more time his mother insisted, "Bobby, we have to go. Come now!"

"But, Mom" he pleaded, *"he has one more move!"*

Many of us fight onward in situations where a wiser, more seasoned mind would see the value in yielding. Why do we contemptuously snub the obvious? Why do we

---

Soften your heart.

sometimes deny the inevitable? Why does our pomposity occasionally rule us?

Defiance leaps from what Jesus called hardness of heart. Hardness of heart shares the same root as pride and arrogance, and Jesus often challenged his listeners to overcome it. Prideful contempt, he insisted, would keep people blinded to the riches God had planned for them.

Jesus likened hardness of heart to yeast. Just a tiny little bit spreads quickly throughout an entire ball of dough. Jesus counseled his followers to be on guard against the yeast of pride, which creates only unhappiness and emptiness.

It's not a death sentence to discover pride and arrogance in yourself, only destructive to persist in them. Contemplate yourself. Recognize the speck of contempt in your heart, and consider the various ways it can spread unhappiness and ineffectiveness through you. Then turn and grow in a safer direction.

A Rhetorical Question

Sometimes the words of people can stick you like a sharp fork. A national educational firm considered hiring me to develop a children's paper-and-pencil personality assessment tool. A former client referred me to the CEO, who wanted to interview me personally before granting me the contract.

He was one cagey dude. He stared at me hard, was quite humorless, and seemed intent on intimidating me. It was working. The coup de grâce, however, came when he was reviewing my credentials. He looked at me and said, "Twelve years of experience as a counselor, eh?"

"Yes, sir," I replied.

"Let me ask you something," he said as he leaned toward me. "Is that 'twelve years of experience or *one year of experience twelve times*?"

I felt as though I were getting pounded, jabbed, and gouged by one of the Three Stooges! I later found out it was a rhetorical question meant to test me. He didn't really care about the answer, but he asked me that question to see how I'd respond.

I don't remember how I answered, but it must have been good enough. I got the contract. What troubled me

You're fully equipped for leadership.

was that it was a great question. It was a great *rhetorical* question because it made me reassess my value from a new perspective. It made me weigh myself with fresh scales. It made me examine my sense of worth with a brighter spotlight. I'm still not sure I know the answer.

Jesus asked many kinds of questions. In most cases I don't think he really wanted answers. The questions were rhetorical ones, and he knew the answers. He wanted to prompt people to think.

Let me ask you a rhetorical question for a specific purpose: *How much more information do you need to lead?* The fact is, very little. What you need are passion and heart. Courage and dreams. You can ask as many questions about leadership as you like, but in the end you have enough to lead right now. Stop asking questions, and go! Lead in the simple things, and the world will follow you.

LOOK FOR THESE OTHER BOOKS IN THE ANCIENT WISDOM FOR MODERN BUSINESS SERIES...

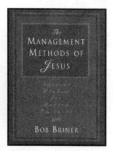

The Management Methods of Jesus

Insight on tough business topics from the man whose organization is more than two thousand years old and still expanding — Jesus of Nazareth. His teachings offer some of the wisest, most compelling advice on making a business successful and lucrative. There is also information on public relations, recruiting and hiring, communication, ethics, and more.

0-7852-7681-5 • Hardcover • 128 pages

The People Skills of Jesus

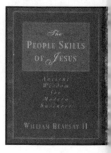

The second in the series, this book is a study of the relationship skills of the greatest "people person" of all time — Jesus himself. Beausay skillfully shows how Jesus handled all manner of personalities in his daily activities and gave us a perfect model to follow in our relationships with others.

0-7852-7164-3 • Hardcover • 128 pages